THE MOON, COME TO EARTH

The moon, come to earth

DISPATCHES FROM LISBON * Philip Graham

THE UNIVERSITY OF CHICAGO PRESS   Chicago and London

PHILIP GRAHAM is the author of two short story collec-
tions, *The Art of the Knock* and *Interior Design*, and a novel,
How to Read an Unwritten Language. He is also the coauthor
(with Alma Gottlieb) of two memoirs of Africa, *Parallel
Worlds* and the forthcoming *Braided Worlds*. Graham teaches
at the University of Illinois–Urbana-Champaign and at the
Vermont College of Fine Arts, and he is a founding editor,
and the fiction editor, of the literary/arts journal *Ninth Letter*.

The University of Chicago Press, Chicago 60637
The University of Chicago Press, Ltd., London
© 2009 by Philip Graham
All rights reserved. Published 2009
Printed in the United States of America

17 16 15 14 13 12 11 10 09   1 2 3 4 5

ISBN-13: 978-0-226-30514-1   (cloth)
ISBN-13: 978-0-226-30515-8   (paper)
ISBN-10: 0-226-30514-7   (cloth)
ISBN-10: 0-226-30515-5   (paper)

Library of Congress Cataloging-in-Publication Data

Graham, Philip, 1951–
   The moon, come to Earth : dispatches from Lisbon / Philip
Graham.
      p. cm.
   Includes bibliographical references and index.
   ISBN-13: 978-0-226-30514-1 (cloth : alk. paper)
   ISBN-13: 978-0-226-30515-8 (pbk. : alk. paper)
   ISBN-10: 0-226-30514-7 (cloth : alk. paper)
   ISBN-10: 0-226-30515-5 (pbk. : alk. paper) 1. Lisbon
(Portugal)—Description and travel. 2. Lisbon (Portugal)—
Anecdotes. 3. Graham, Philip, 1951—Travel—Portugal—
Lisbon. I. Title.
   DP776.G73 2009
   914.6904'44—dc22

                                              2009010513

♾ The paper used in this publication meets the minimum
requirements of the American National Standard for
Information Sciences—Permanence of Paper for Printed
Library Materials, ANSI Z39.48-1992.

FOR HANNAH

CONTENTS

Acknowledgments

I would like to thank Alma Gottlieb, Hannah Gottlieb-Graham, Nathaniel Gottlieb-Graham, John Griswold, Robin Hemley, David Jauss, Roy Kesey, Michele Morano, Kirin Narayan, and Sue Silverman, as well as my editors at *McSweeney's*, John Warner and Christopher Monks, and my editor at the University of Chicago, David Brent, for their careful and helpful readings of these dispatches and for their support. I am also grateful to the University of Illinois, Urbana-Champaign, for a sabbatical release, Humanities Release Time, and Research Board support of my year abroad.

Muito obrigado to so many friends who welcomed my family with such grace and care to their country: Luís Batalha, Rachel Caiano, Maria José Coelho and Sara Coelho, Catarina Costa, Maria Helena dá Mesquita, Barbara Doria, Pedro Faria, Sónia Fragoso, Mick Greer, Graça Margarido, Helena Martins, Jacinto Lucas Pires, Nuno Porto, Fernanda Pratas, Eurizanda Bemilde de Fátima Martins Semedo dos Reis, Sandra Robalo, Clara Saraiva, Jorge Simões, Gonçalo Tavares, Susana Viegas, and Rui Zink.

Many thanks to Bruno Peinado for permission to use the photo, by Gonçalo Fonseca, of his artwork *Sans Titre, Globule Ubiquity Vibrations*, 2006.

To my wife, son, daughter, I have no words that could adequately express the thanks and love you deserve in this life we share.

Most of these dispatches first appeared, some in slightly different form, at *McSweeney's Internet Tendency*, as part of the series "Philip Graham Spends a Year in Lisbon."

I DON'T KNOW WHY
I LOVE LISBON

The grilled sardines lying on my plate are much larger than those stunted little things packed in tins that go by the same name in the United States, and their eye sockets stare up at the ceiling, where hanging light fixtures are shaped like gourds. The aroma of sardines led me here, the scent sharp at first as it hit the nose (perhaps too sharp) until the smoky complexities took over, akin—at least for me—to a bouquet of wine. I take another sip from my glass of *vinho verde* and peer up at the small square of the TV perched on a high shelf beside the restaurant's open door. The screen displays a smaller green rectangle of a soccer pitch, with even smaller figures of players racing back and forth.

Across the table in this typically narrow and crowded Lisbon *tasca* (mirroring the long and narrow streets of the Bairro Alto, an appealing neighborhood mix of funky shops and clothes drying on balconies), my nineteen-year-old ponytailed son, Nathaniel, sits enthralled by the beginning of this World Cup game: Portugal against the Netherlands. We've both caught some of the local *futebol* passion through a sneaky process of cultural osmosis, because there's been no escape from the billboards, metro announcements, and TV ads celebrating the World Cup games. For only the second time in history, a Portuguese team has made it to the second round, and tonight they're fighting for a berth in the third round, the final eight. My normally sports-averse son is actually interested, maybe because I mentioned a few days ago that Jack Kemp had once denounced soccer, on the floor of the House of Representatives, as a "socialist sport." It's a well-worn tactic—as a kid, Nathaniel finally ate his broccoli after my wife and I told him that the first President Bush hated the stuff. But Nathaniel also has a real gift for geometry, and maybe that's what secretly attracts him as he keeps his eyes on the TV—the constant reshuffling of the players' patterns on the pitch.

Already in the first minutes the Dutch team has begun some serious harsh play, enough to draw two yellow warning cards, in what seems like an attempt to intimidate Portugal from the get-go. Nathaniel shuffles nervously in his seat, glances at me. On the flight over, I'd made the mistake of reading aloud passages about fan hooliganism from Franklin Foer's marvelous *How Soccer Explains the World*. At the time, a description of one soccer thug's arm that "folds around in a direction that would defy a healthy network of joints and tendons" made for some good head-slapping, eye-rolling camaraderie on a long flight, but now I'm regretting it, because I've had to nag Nathaniel all day to get him to watch tonight's game in a public place. I try listening in on the conversations of the people sitting at neighboring tables in an attempt to catch their mood, but spoken Portuguese—with all its succulent *oo*s and *oosh*es, *oish*es and *aows*—still glides by too quickly for me, even after years of tutoring in the language.

Still, I'm happy just to be here. I love Lisbon.

I don't know why I love Lisbon. But I jumped at the chance to participate in the international short-story conference being held here this week. What a gig—all I have to do is give a reading of one of my stories, manage as a panelist to say something remotely intelligent about literary editing, and collaborate on a video essay on the conference with my technically astute son, and then I get to wander around one of my favorite cities. When I'm walking its stone-cobbled streets, catching glimpses here and there of the bordering Tejo River, or taking in, from a vista on one of the city's hills, the glorious staggered topography of the white buildings and their salmon-colored tile roofs, I feel that I'm also traveling some interior landscape, that those streets are leading to a place inside myself I haven't yet located.

Our neighbors cheer and our waitress swirls an impromptu dance —Maniche, the Portuguese midfielder, has scored the first goal, a beautifully aimed strike that in replay has an inevitability about it, as the ball slices through the shifting open spaces of a tumble of defenders in a direct elegant line to the corner of the net. His long dark hair plastered in sweat against the sides of his exultant face, Maniche wades through an eruption of his teammates' joy at the seemingly impossible having been so artfully accomplished.

I take another sip of the house wine, watch the continuing replays of the goal. I don't know why I feel at home here, but I have a theory. My family on my father's side is Scottish and Catholic. Not a popular mixture back in the home country, which is why my dad's parents, cousins, aunts, and uncles emigrated en masse to New York in 1927—typical bad timing, two years before the Depression, but that's another story. Why, when, and where, I've often wondered, did my family shed its Presbyterian roots?

On the banks of the Douro River in northern Portugal, there's a port-wine vineyard called the Quinta dos Malvedos. In 1820, two Graham brothers who lived in Oporto, William and John (my grandfather's first name was John, and my father's, William!), worked for a trading company based in Glasgow (where my family comes from!), and they founded that *quinta*. Couldn't my father's family, almost two hundred years ago, have raised grapes on the banks of the Douro River and eventually converted to Catholicism? And if some returned to Scotland (black sheep, certainly—why else leave a vineyard?), then back in Glasgow they paid the piper for their unwelcome faith.

It's probably all bullshit, but I hold that shred of possibility to help explain why the full-throated, plaintive twists of a fado song can sometimes bring me close to tears, or why Portuguese *saudade*—a complicated feeling that combines sorrow, longing, and regret, laced perhaps with a little mournful pleasure—fits so easily in my own emotional baggage. There's something beyond romantic delusion, something deeper, that beckons me: it's a genetic thing, a need to cross the centuries and return home, if only for a little while. I'm sure any Scottish genealogy service could easily burst this fragile bubble, which is why I'll never consult one.

Cries of despair rise around us. The Dutch team has gone a little crazy in its attempt to even the score. Cristiano Ronaldo, a team star, is the victim of a vicious kick and is forced to leave the game. The baby-faced player cries as he exits, which make his features appear even younger. Those damn Dutch—they made a little kid cry!

Minutes later Cristiano's teammate Costinha returns Dutch fire with a nasty foul—his second of the game—and he's ejected with a red card. Yet for all the rough stuff on the screen, the Portuguese maintain their good spirits. Nathaniel relaxes, nods at me: we're far from English-soccer-fan hooliganism here.

During halftime, I continue to scrape the delicious sardines down to their spinal columns with great care and deliberation. I know I can't make these babies last until the end of the game, so I order more wine, and if the match goes into overtime there's always dessert to order and slowly savor.

Once the game resumes, it threatens to become a brawl. The referee is in over his head, and he starts throwing out so many yellow cards that the commentators on TV seem to have lost count. His attempts to control the roughhousing only further incite the players on both teams, and the foul fest continues. Even the Portuguese goalkeeper, Ricardo, draws a yellow card. It's become the kind of game that could set off any number of silently ticking heart attacks.

Nathaniel starts throwing those looks at me again, but now they're just a joke, because it's clear that our amiable Portuguese neighbors take it all in lightly while tucking into their sardines and grilled pork ribs, and I feel a rush of affection for these people I don't know. Yes, this is an important game, a crucial game, but I sense no barely suppressed rage beneath the surface. My neighbors seem to have their heads on straight: they're enjoying the game, win or lose. I *like* these people. I'm even happier that Lisbon will soon be my home for the coming year, though it still seems more an imagined future than one that's rapidly approaching. In a month I'll return with my family, and my wife, Alma, will ply her anthropological skills studying Cape Verdeans, our daughter, Hannah, will start the sixth grade at a Portuguese school that's a five-minute walk from our apartment, and I'll finish writing a few books that have been begging for extended time and attention. I'll finally learn Portuguese—because isn't it true that simply breathing Lisbon air helps in memorizing the irregular conjugations of the preterit?

Now that we've passed the midpoint of the second half, the Dutch are deep into need-to-score desperation, and maybe their chance will come—the Portuguese team has been a man down since Costinha was ejected, and fatigue is setting in. Suddenly, Figo, the team captain, writhes on the ground, his hands covering his face, and everyone around us gasps at this possible further loss.

After the Dutch player Boulahrouz is ejected with a red card, Figo makes a remarkable recovery. On replay it's clear that Figo was only lightly brushed on the chest by Boulahrouz's elbow during a tight run for the ball and then, after half of a tenth of a split second's hesitation, Figo reared his head back and began his face-clutching and wriggling dramatics, pouring it on for the benefit of the referee. It's such flagrant fakery that we all cluck approval at the theatrics. After all, Boulahrouz was the one who injured Cristiano in the first half, and we're satisfied with this imprecisely accomplished justice.

Soon two more red cards cast a player on each side out of the game. Both teams are now, incredibly, playing with only nine men on the field. Somehow, the Portuguese manage in the final minutes to tough out their one-goal lead, and then the *tasca* crowd cheers and the waiters and waitresses rush out to the street to dance on the cobbled stones and sing a souped-up version of the national anthem.

Nathaniel and I wend our way through the dancing streets down to the subway, and while we wait the Portuguese seem a bit surprised to me, as if they secretly didn't believe they'd win this game. Perhaps unrestrained expressions of joy aren't exactly local tender, perhaps worries already abound because the heavily favored English team will be playing Portugal in the next round. Then the subway cars arrive packed with revelers, many sporting goofy porkpie hats in the colors of the Portuguese flag, and again I get a sense from these celebrants—a slight, barely perceptible hesitation here and there—that any happiness leaving *saudade* behind may be uncharted territory.

Nathaniel and I reach our stop, and as we begin our climb up the stairs to the street, the tiled walls echo with countless honking car horns from the street above. Outside, we watch the broad avenue packed with a traffic jam of delirious fans hanging from car windows or just managing to balance on the roofs, waving flags and shouting victory: *Portugal! Portugal!* Maybe it's not so hard for *saudade* to take a temporary backseat after all. Back in our hotel room, I lean out the window and listen to the horns and cheers echoing off the same streets I'll be wandering in the coming year while I try to discover why I love Lisbon. I give in to my own glee, and for hours into the night the whole city sings.

SO WHO SAYS OBJECTS ARE INANIMATE?

The apartment is larger, the rooms more spacious, than I expected. Something about the clean line of the walls seems typically European to me, though I'm not quite sure what I mean by that. Windows in every room—there'll be lots of light, even though now the sun is low on the horizon of this neighborhood perched above the monuments of Belém. I'm not crazy about our location on the ground floor, but three of the rooms open to a patio that's part of the apartment complex's private garden, and if I crane my neck out through the living-room window, I can see a sliver of the far side of the Tejo River. So this is the space where my wife and daughter and I will be living for a year. I want to say something out loud, but how do you introduce yourself to a new apartment?

Somehow we'll make these rooms our own, breathe into them something of ourselves. Now, though, after a long haul of flights that has finally deposited us in Lisbon, it's a daunting prospect to even consider springing our clothes from their luggage prisons and relocating them in new rooms, new dresser drawers and closets. An unsettling time, this settling in, and we barely hear the rental manager as he gives us lots of apartment advice in quite good English—a blessing, since our Portuguese is not up to par.

Still, we have enough energy to pick up some essentials at a nearby store, and on our return Hannah summons a deep reserve of eleven-year-old life force and begins organizing her room. Alma and I listlessly examine the furniture and the pictures on the walls, which all exude a cool aesthetic intelligence. The sun is setting and so we check the lights. In the kitchen, there's a raft of flat switches set together, and together Alma and I start to press them.

The lights shut off and an alarm begins a steady, aptly alarming whine. "Why are the lights out?" Hannah calls from her room, and Alma moans, "Oh, no, what did we do?" We start pressing the switches in various frantic combinations, but the damage has been done and we quickly give it up.

Alma runs down the hall to search for any helpful neighbor while I stay behind with Hannah and search for something, anything, in the apartment—I'll even accept help from the little scuffs of lint and dust in the corners if necessary—that might suggest an unlikely solution to our troubles: a magical Reverso button that erases blunders would be ideal, but I'm having trouble finding any help in this apartment that grows darker and darker. On and on, the alarm screeches, and I realize we've added this current mess to a family tradition of First-Day Settling-In Disasters. Like the last time we lived in Africa.

We'd just arrived in the Beng village of Asagbé, in Côte d'Ivoire, where Alma had been doing her anthropological fieldwork off and on since 1979, and during the punishing twenty miles of dirt road that was the last leg of our journey, too many golden memories of that route returned to me: two cracked chassis, four shattered windshields, and more flattened tires than I cared to recount. I had another problem with this road: I'd once taken a nasty tumble off a bike, and some villagers believed not only that spirits were responsible but that they were still possibly gunning for me. I would have preferred navigating the unreliable rural bus system for this three-month stay, but we'd brought our then six-year-old son, Nathaniel, with us and needed guaranteed quick access to medical help in case of an emergency.

After arriving in the village we quickly settled into our new two-room mud-brick house, but the next morning we woke to the car alarm's unnerving howl, a rhythmic pulse of unhappiness that wouldn't stop no matter how I fiddled with the ignition and poked at the engine. All the rattling on the dirt road the day before must have loosened the car-alarm thingy, but just where *was* that thingy?

Our friends in the compound gathered, eyes fearful, and were soon joined by a crowd of villagers. Still the siren screamed, and an animist priest in the next compound called for a chicken to sacrifice so he could appease any displeased spirits, who are the Beng people's usual go-to explanation for any confounding trouble.

No amount of poking about the engine and its mysterious wiry, hoselike whatchamacallits produced any solution, and I cursed myself for my cozy middle-class American ignorance of mechanical basics. I wasn't going to solve this, and the car alarm might eventually run down the battery. The only chance was to turn around and return the way we came, to the small town of M'Bahiakro at the other end of those nasty twenty miles of dirt road. There, any number of itinerant mechanics would be happy to take on the challenge.

Down we drove, a four-wheel caterwauling headache, and I found myself able to summon some sympathy for the car—it was simply registering shock at the job we'd be asking it to do in the next three months. "I know, I know," I whispered to the dashboard, with a glance around to make sure no one was listening, "the road here is tough—hey, *life* here is tough—but can't you just suck it up?" But I was also pissed: that damn alarm was screeching out our arrival to any interested spirits who may not have forgotten me. "So you didn't like the road the first time?" I asked, sotto voce. "Well, now you're getting a bellyful of it, aren't you?"

The apartment is so dark now I can barely see. Thank God we bought matches at the little shop for the gas stove, because now I can use them to search for whatever it is I'm looking for. Why aren't our neighbors standing in a curious crowd outside our open front door? Where is that helpful neighbor Alma went searching for? Helpful Neighbors are always important. They certainly were when our last First-Day Settling-In Disaster occurred. We were preparing to cook our first meal in a little country-house vacation rental on the outside slope of Sete Cidades, an extinct volcano on the Portuguese island of São Miguel, in the Azores. I wanted to rinse off some of the plates from the cabinet, and with a simple twist of the hot-water tap I produced a stomach-dropping crunch of a noise from the sink, just before water spurted out of the pipes below.

A quick wet inspection told me I was out of my league here. (Where *is* my proficiency when it comes to the mechanical, besides being able to make a scissors snip back and forth?) While Alma, Hannah, and Nathaniel commandeered the mop, pail, and towels, I ran to our neighbors, who I knew could phone the housekeeper. My rudimentary Portuguese at least got across "Emergency!" and when João arrived he made a great show of pretending that he, too, wasn't out of his league, but the water continued spreading across the kitchen tiles and onto the stone floor of the dining room. I had the creeping feeling that, stone or no, we were in danger of floating out to sea.

Just then, a knock at the door, and an American couple made their unlikely appearance—they were friends of the owners and hadn't known the house had been rented for the week. The husband, it turned out, was a plumber licensed in New Jersey, New York, and Connecticut.

Alma finally returns with our latest "plumber," a harried fellow from the third floor whose poor English perversely complements our poor Portuguese. He locates the fuse box while I stand behind him with a match in the darkness, and with a flip here, a flip there, we're back in business. We offer embarrassed thanks in our newly lit apartment.

Alma and I are completely wired now. So we join Hannah in plunging into our suitcases, and while we empty and arrange the contents into their new nooks and crannies, I wonder what set off our First-Day Disaster today. Did the unfamiliar sounds of English echoing off the walls unnerve our Lisbon apartment?

Of course, there are perfectly mechanical explanations for all our Disasters—a weak joint in a pipe, a sudden electrical overload in an apartment left vacant for a few months, a car alarm nearly jostled to death by miles of washboard dirt road. But I know more than a few African diviners who'd smile at such a thought. All that is simply the effect, they'd say, merely a secondary physical manifestation of a hidden, psychic cause.

I contemplate the notion that no matter where you are in the world, you'll find objects—so-called mere things—that, just like people, are skittish in the face of newcomers or a novel situation. While people have doubts and silent screams of protest at too much change (too much!), machines will simply break down. And perhaps they do this to give us the opportunity to prove that we can and will repair them, that change is also marked by a return to wholeness.

*

I'm still thinking about this a couple of days later when I read about
the opening of Lisboa Mágica, a six-day street festival of more than
twenty magicians. A perfect treat for Hannah, who has been won-
derfully patient, sitting and reading a book beside us while Alma
and I navigate the various unfamiliar bureaucratic mazes of banking,
cell-phone plans, Internet access, and cable TV (gotta have the Disney Channel). We've been mostly trotting out our faltering Portuguese, and sometimes making complex financial arrangements in a
language one barely understands feels like riding white-water rapids
using a teaspoon for an oar.

We all need a diversion, so why not take in the likes of Flicto, Dr.
Chango, or Mad Martin? After our first night, I'm in a magic mood,
and there are lots of shows to choose from—seven or more a day, at
various downtown street corners and plazas. Under the shadow of a
statue of the great poet Luís de Camões, they perform; in the Rossio,
where executions of the Inquisition once took place, they perform;
in the Praça do Comércio, where a tidal wave during the earthquake
of 1755 drowned thousands, they perform; in the Largo do Chiado,
across the street from Fernando Pessoa's favorite café, they perform.

We decide to take in more than a few shows, and, as we join each
semicircled crowd, I can see that the Portuguese make a good audience—polite but appreciative, compliant when prompted by a magician to participate. But there are always a few who don't pour so easily into that mold—an unshaven old man here, an overtaxed mother
there—who display a sometimes loud and opinionated crankiness.
Even if I can't completely follow what they're saying, the content is
clear enough: Now *that's* a good trick. How in the world *did* he do
that? Him, he *really* should practice more.

The range of magicians puts the "mixed" in mixed bag: some
barely rise above the level of birthday-party entertainment while
others seek and receive our awe. Flicto, a Spanish magician, wears
an outfit—tall dark hat and colorful floppy clothes—that takes him
halfway to the realm of clown, giving him a persona silly enough to
weather his indifferent skills. The English magician J.J. likes to balance on a misanthropic edge, at one point threatening to break both
legs and one arm of a small child who keeps running in front of his

act. Ray Francas, from Argentina, is wonderful with the kids, teasingly winning over each of his chosen helpers. And rubber-faced Dr. Chango, from Spain, flips a lit cigarette into his mouth and then amazes us with what he can do with the smoke.

We see too many rope tricks, too many scarf tricks. Personality, *lots* of personality, is needed to grease some of these old standards. Even so, it's all good fun, and on the metro line back home Alma, Hannah, and I chat up our favorite moments, but it's magic with a small *m*, the semblance of invisible power but not the power itself, magic without the eerie feeling that the uncanny is being held in difficult check. Certainly nothing like the weird energy we encountered our first night in Lisbon, when the apartment—awakened from a few months of empty slumber and perhaps alarmed at our alien presence, our own suppressed fears of the new—seemed to greet us with a yawp of surprise.

365 DAYS OF PORK SURPRISE

Alma doesn't eat pork. It's not exactly a religious commitment—her offhand atheism sometimes shocks even little old watered-down-pantheist me. And I don't think it's about ethnic culinary solidarity, since nearly all our nonvegetarian Jewish friends eat pork. Sure, we observe Passover and mainly ignore Easter (except for the baskets of chocolate bunnies). We celebrate both Hanukkah and Christmas (double dibs on presents for our grateful children). But these are secularized observances, done more to instill in our son and daughter memories of some sense of ritual, of tradition. I think Alma's pork prohibition, a fairly recent choice, is the line in the sand of her Jewish identity, maybe even some secret penance for marrying a Scottish-American Catholic (however irrevocably lapsed).

Back in the United States, pork avoidance is a relatively simple procedure, like viewing distant storm clouds and having all the time in the world to head for shelter. But here in Portugal just saying no to pork can be the trickiest of culinary obstacle courses, and only the strong survive.

Our first full day in Lisbon, we begin the initial steps of a gallop (a molasseslike gallop) through various Portuguese bureaucracies to establish our new household. Hannah is patient through it all, reading a book or drawing in her notepad, so Alma and I, tired and crabby, decide to reward her when we come upon a Chinese restaurant a few doors down from our new bank: an ideal treat of familiar food. Along with our meals, we order a plate of rice, and the waitress comes to our table with a neatly shaped oval mound that's flecked, we see upon closer inspection, with tiny cubes of ham.

Alma is hungry after all our various treks, so she painstakingly separates with the prongs of her fork those offending pink pieces from the white grains of rice, choosing to ignore the thought that there might be a leftover glaze of hamishness on the rice itself. If she can't see it, it's magically no longer ham. I happen to love the stuff and so dig in happily. Alma jokes that if this meal is any indication, the year ahead will be a challenge. My wife is graced with a generous soul, and her anthropological training easily allows her to give the Portuguese a break. Besides, she has a soft spot for the values behind placing recycling bins every few blocks in our neighborhood, and she was delighted to hear that in Portugal nearly all local produce is organically grown. And then there's the seafood, the wonderful seafood . . .

A few days later, as our dear Portuguese friend Helena guides us through the labyrinth of the vast Continente mall complex, I find in the meat section of the supermarket a corner devoted to *alheiras*— sausages without pork. They were invented by Portuguese Jews in the fifteenth century who were among the roughly 10 percent of the population who had been forced to convert to Christianity or leave. If you stayed and still secretly held to your beliefs, not eating sausages was a dead giveaway, *dead* being the active word here, since the Inquisition was a powerful force. So Jews living a clandestine religious life came up with stealth sausages filled with various spices, chicken meat, lamb, game meat, whatever was needed to mimic the taste of pork.

Alheiras in a grocery, whodathunkit? Yet here at least six varieties shine beneath the counter lights, so I immediately pick up a pack of Alheiras Caça. Alma can finally eat Portuguese pork-free sausage, a culinary item so oxymoronic that it'll surely add zip to the taste. And I can substitute *alheiras* for the pork in some of my favorite Portuguese meals, and cook squid stuffed with *alheiras*, or a *cataplana* with clams, potatoes, and *alheiras* . . . ah, the possibilities.

The following evening I struggle with the meal I'm preparing, because the *alheiras* are falling apart in a sizzling mix of garlic, onions, tomato, zucchini, and potatoes. The hearty chunks I'd envisioned have vanished, and I give one fragile lump a taste—it's pungent, vinegary. Alheiras Caça—what does *caça* mean, anyway? I turn down the heat, making a silent note to hurry back, because I can get lost in a Portuguese dictionary. Simply flipping through a few pages, I find that *estou de maré alta* means to be in a good mood. *Maré alta* means high tide, which is an apt metaphor for a country whose past greatness is based on maritime exploits. I briefly run through a fantasy of saying this and having a Portuguese acquaintance stare and then laugh at me. Here's a better phrase: *claro com água*, a nice way to say "crystal clear," though I can't imagine much of anything in the language being crystal clear to me, at least not for a while. Then I find this intriguing trio of words: *escrever* means to write, *escrevinhar* means to scribble, and an *escrevinhador* is a hack writer.

I finally make it to *caça*: game meat. So maybe that's why the sausage (or what used to look like sausage—I'm back in the kitchen now and staring at a meatlike mush clinging to everything else in the pan) tastes, er, gamy. But is that all there is in the sausage? I rummage around in the garbage bag, find a list-of-ingredients tag, and discover that *carne do porco* is the first listed ingredient.

What's this? Inquisition-brand *alheiras*? What a mean thing to do! Or it may not be malicious, merely clueless. I remember once taking a flight on a Portuguese airline during which the flight attendants served ham sandwiches for lunch—no other option. The Portuguese don't seem to be able to think about pork as a "problematic" meat; it's too much a part of daily life. I've read somewhere that every part of a pig is used for some sort of recipe in Portuguese cooking, and that pork dishes are an integral part of many religious festivals. Since Paleolithic times, when stone statues of pigs dotted the countryside, pork has been the culture's culinary obsession (and obsession is something I bow down to, in celebration and fear—a hefty proportion of the people in my fiction are gripped by personal passions that in various measures both fulfill and twist them). But putting pork in an "alheiras" sausage? That seems wrong, wronger than clueless.

The entire meal is suffused with the stuff, there's no way to salvage it, and just then Alma and Hannah return home (yes, home, even if only a handful of days' worth of home so far), happy with the results of their shopping expedition, hungry from all their walking about the city. There's no way I can wipe off the gooey *alheiras* from the chunks of potato and zucchini, the slivers of garlic and onion, and we don't have anything else in the refrigerator for dinner.

"What's for dinner?" Alma asks, and when I say, "Alheiras," she grins at the prospect with such anticipation (she loves the story of the cleverness of her ancestors) that I can't work the words "but pork, pork" out of my mouth as she leans over the pan, takes a sample spoonful, and compliments the chef.

I move like a sleepwalker as I set the table—this is terrible; I cannot knowingly let my wife eat pork, but she just did and she'll be so disappointed if I tell her the *alheiras* have pork; I must have picked the wrong kind; I wonder if maybe I can find a pigless version and serve her that later and no one will be the wiser—

At the table, more compliments. I swallow the *alheiras* along with my shame. I can't tell her, and I know that if I don't go to hell for this then I'm going to pay for it in another life, if I'm even *allowed* another life. I can't ever tell her. Ever. I'll never tell her.

I tell her. My vows of silence never last more than an hour or so. I'm not worth a damn at keeping secrets. So, later that evening, with some hemming and hawing ("Do you know what *caça* means, by the way?" I ask her), I finally confess in the softest, most contrite voice I can muster, ready to be blasted to perdition. Alma gives me one of those especially powerful, withering looks made all the more effective because she has large, beautiful eyes. She pauses a beat, then says she'll add this to the long list of things she needs to forgive me for.

Two days later we realize that there's not much in the fridge. (We've located a local grocery that sells fresh meat and fish, but it's a long walk away.) It's time to scrounge. There are some noodles, and a pack of hot dogs Alma had bought for Hannah. (She'd examined every available brand for telltale signs of *porco* until she finally came upon a package of slim wieners without the dreaded word.)

Now, though, before chopping up the franks and adding them to some pasta, Alma reflects on the *alheiras* incident, and, after an utterly deserved reproachful look at me, she checks each ingredient in the dictionary *before* cooking. She doesn't have to look far: *suino*, the first ingredient, is defined as "pig, hog." The third ingredient, *gordura do suino*, is pig fat.

So lesson learned: check the label, check it with the best dictionary you can find. (I'm beginning to wonder if the *caça*—"game meat" —of the *alheiras* is actually wild boar.) Perhaps a thesaurus of pork terms is available, because one should never assume that there isn't anything such as pork ice cream, pork breakfast cereal, or pork reconstituted and hardened into lawn chairs, or worse, forks and knives.

The next evening, we're all sitting at a table in a snazzy restaurant in the Chiado neighborhood. Little *pratos* of appetizers appear—green olives in various sizes and hues, savory cheese, thick crusty bread, and a circular arrangement of what must seem to Alma a toxic-waste dump of thinly sliced *presunto*. I'm on my game and, without a word, deftly ease it down the table away from her, and as she reads the menu I remind her that *entrecote* means pork ribs. Yet what, really, will all our precautions accomplish? I remember reading years ago that there are no true vegetarians, since the air we breathe is filled with microscopic particles of dust, pollen, bits of dead insects, and, if you're walking past a McDonald's, microscopic morsels of hamburger. If this is true, imagine the multifarious pork products that must drift through the air currents of Lisbon.

But I can't tell Alma this, ever. I'll never tell her.

ALCHEMY: FROM A RUBE
TO A LOCAL

Our three tickets rest on the desk beside the exact change I gave the ticket clerk, and outside I can hear the echoing clack of the train approaching the station. From the realm of his glass box the clerk gazes down at it all, then stares at the computer screen before him, and then, turning his head (at such a leisurely pace I can imagine hearing the shifting of his neck muscles), he regards a posted train schedule on the wall, lines and lines and lines of little numbers.

We need to catch this train. My normally vivacious daughter stands outside on the platform with Alma, and though Hannah appears placid, she's deep in the land of stir-crazy, overwhelmed by our recent move and a language she doesn't understand, in a funk about the temporary loss of her friends back home. So Alma and I have come up with the band-aid of a movie that's in English, not dubbed. And there will be Portuguese subtitles, which will give Alma and me some needed language practice. All we have to do is catch this train.

The train comes to a stop, and there's a hiss of opening doors. I can hear behind me the scrape and scuff of people stepping off, getting on, while the ticket clerk again turns to gaze upon the three tickets (and I try to will forward the careful pivot of his spinal column). Once again he looks at the money I gave him, which he has already counted. I need those tickets—there are no sales on the train, we've heard. I can't read his face, it's blank—no confusion, no boredom, no squint of malice. Everyone outside has boarded, though the doors remain open. There's still a chance that we could catch this train, with a quick snatch of the tickets and a leap through the open door. Wanting to say something encouraging, I painstakingly construct in my mind the sentence *Faz favor, o Senor, pode dar-me os meus bilhetes?*—Please, sir, can you give me my tickets?—but I don't want to slow his deliberations by any mangled pronunciation or grammar.

Another examination of the schedule on the wall. Another long gaze at the money on the desk. The doors of the train close. Only then does his hand slowly rise with the tickets, an echo of the deliberate pace of the train pulling away from the station, as if his gesture were attached to its departure. Though his face remains an indifferent mask, I take in the reflection of my shocked face in the window of the glass booth.

Without a word, I accept the tickets and walk out to the platform, where Alma and Hannah stand, disappointed, in the sun. Alma quickly consults the movie and train timetable while I console Hannah and try to explain what I think happened. "We're in luck!" Alma says, relieved. We can make the next showing, easy.

When the next train finally arrives, we take a smooth, swift ride along tracks parallel to the Tejo River—beautiful views, but I can't stop pushing the replay button on that encounter with the ticket clerk. His behavior seemed intentional, but why? Had I insulted him by some ritual behavior I hadn't performed, some local knowledge that would be obvious to anyone living here but invisible to me? I need to figure this out, because his glass booth is parked in our neighborhood train station and there are surely encounters with this fellow in our future.

It's always the little things that crowd you when you're new. How much—or not—to tip. Why are some seats on the bus different colors. How to start the damn dishwasher or light the hot-water heater. How to quickly tell the difference between a five- and ten-centavo piece when a line of people behind you wait to buy their own morning paper. It's like existing in an adult amalgam of babytude and toddlerdom, where life is not yet a walk but a waddle. I remember this feeling from years back, during our long first months of village life in Africa: Who knew that sniffing a simmering pot of food and complimenting the aroma was a terrible insult? Who knew that whistling in the forest annoyed certain spirits?

I'm already working hard to keep on point with my best behavior here. Before we left for Lisbon, Alma and I studied a couple of books on Portuguese manners and customs, and two short entries waved their flags directly at me: the Portuguese aren't crazy, apparently, about loud sneezing or loud laughing. At home, at the sound of my rhythmic "eh, eh, eh" preamble to a sneeze, my children place their hands over their ears and close their eyes. (Why the eyes? I wonder. There are no auditory nerves in the cornea.) Hannah claims she has heard me sneeze from across the street at a friend's house. I can usually control this—with enough warning the explosion can be suppressed within normal bounds. Laughing, however, is an entirely different matter. My booming laugh simply happens, a guffaw I'm not aware of until I've already guffawed it. It's nearly instantaneous plug 'n' play: amuse me and then run for the hills.

We arrive at the movie theater, which is part of a two-storied mall, which in turn is housed in the base of one of the largest soccer stadiums in Lisbon: the nested dolls of a Portuguese consumer's paradise. So we stand in line and I take out my change to examine and finally it clicks: the ten-centavo coin is smaller than the five-centavo coin. Ah, like the dime and the nickel, I can remember that, and this triumph is one of those welcome moments when the clueless rube takes another tiny step toward being one of the locals. It's an alchemical process: transforming newcomer dross into another nugget of insider gold.

But when the woman at the counter starts asking me questions I don't understand, there's the rub: show a little local competence and people will assume you know everything else. I stare, she repeats her questions, this time pointing at the sodas and the popcorn machine behind her, and I realize that here in Portugal you buy your snacks together with your ticket. In a moment I've gone from alchemy to Zeno's paradox: a flying arrow, speeding from bow to target, passes first half the distance, then half of that, and so on, with each division of space smaller and smaller so that the arrow never gets to the end. Well, there are a lot of dead and buried souls whose corpses prove that arrows *do* hit their targets, but still I feel Zeno was onto something. In another country, it's those half-steps that'll do you in.

✳

I say, "Com licença"—excuse me—and I say, "Faz favor"—please—and I ask for three tickets and hand him the correct change. And smile. He doesn't seem to remember me—good. He takes out the tickets, counts the money, and then slowly turns his head to examine the schedule posted on the wall, and we're off to the races again. Another gaze to the tickets, another long take on the computer screen, and I can't believe it (not again!)—there's the sound outside of the train approaching. This is not a recurring dream, but it plays like one: the clerk's same glacial attention to who knows what, and then his carefully choreographed bestowal of tickets just as the train pulls away.

I resist any expression of dismay or anger. I'm an American living abroad, after all, and so have the entire sorry record of the Bush administration to live down. I accept the tickets, without comment. I can't resist glancing back before I set out onto the platform, though. His head is down, preoccupied with something. At least he doesn't gloat: I'm already forgotten.

Again Alma and Hannah stand waiting on the platform, disappointed. But what really catches my attention is a man standing a few feet away from them. His look of astonishment as I leave the ticket office registers as something like *Why in the world were you in there?* Then I notice a line of people standing before a green rectangular box attached to the wall outside that immediately comes into focus as a ticket dispenser. (Oh, how could we have walked by this so many times and not seen it?) They're staring at me, too, looks of surprise that say it all: *Are you crazy? Nobody deals with that guy, ever.* And I realize that none of them are queued up for the clerk, just a handful of steps away.

Though we have tickets in hand, Alma and I get in line. We're determined to figure out this machine, because it's a kind of anti-nasty-ticket-taker device. A very *nice* anti-nasty-ticket-taker device, we discover, because it will sell us ten trip fares, and, after a few false starts, we manage to push the right buttons.

So *não faz mal*, as they say—no harm done. We have no pressing engagement downtown, the train ride is air-conditioned and smooth, and we settle into our seats with the contentment that comes from having deciphered a good-sized chunk of local knowledge. I relax and page through my dog-eared copy of *The Book of Disquiet*, by Fernando Pessoa.

He's one of my favorite writers, an odd bird of a poet who identified and named the multiple possibilities of his personality, gave them birth dates and biographies, and allowed them to write, through him, their very different styles of poetry. An entire literary salon met regularly inside him. Actually not an odd bird at all, but the cartographer of what we know about our hidden selves but mostly ignore. He's a Portuguese national hero, and you can buy Fernando Pessoa T-shirts, coffee cups, and key chains almost anywhere in town.

One of Pessoa's alternate selves was Bernardo Soares, a disaffected philosophical sort who worked in an office and the "author" of *The Book of Disquiet*. As the train passes under the impressive soaring curve of the 25 de Abril Bridge, I flip through the pages (it's that kind of book—short, prose-poem-like passages, good for dipping into) and read, "I'm almost convinced that I'm never awake. I'm not sure if I'm not in fact dreaming when I live, and living when I dream, or if dreaming and living are for me intersected, intermingled things that together form my conscious self."

Mulling on a nugget like this could take care of the rest of the ride, but something makes me flip the pages again, and I read, "I have before me, on the slanted surface of the old desk, the two large pages of the ledger, from which I lift my tired eyes and even more tired soul." Pessoa himself worked in an office, was virtually unknown throughout his life, and I can see his now famous face—lean and mustached, wearing thin-rimmed glasses, a hat above—rise from the ledger. Again I press on and search further—I'm not sure why—here and there, until I find "If I lift up my eyes from my thinking, they smart at the sight of the world."

I glance up at the window and see the faint reflection of my own surprised face as I remember the ticket clerk, a few miles of train track safely behind me, and wonder if I've stumbled onto the method behind his madness. What if invisible, convoluted strands of his imagination fill that glassed-in booth, and he sees anyone approaching as an alien unable to breathe his own brand of air? If so, what are a few strangers' missed connections to the unwelcome loss of his dream-state? His reputation has given him the solitude he craves, with the help of an accomplice, that ticket dispenser right outside on the platform. Maybe everyone in the neighborhood gives him wide latitude in that booth, recognizing his artistic disposition, his need to defend an interior domain against all comers. Maybe those looks of shock and surprise I received weren't sympathy for me but for the clerk who'd been interrupted by an insensitive newbie.

I blush, and then an alternate, Pessoa-like voice inside me rises up and says, *Or maybe he's just a pain in the ass.*

So who knows? A dreamer, or trouble that everyone else has learned to avoid? Either way, that ticket machine on the train platform is my new friend. Still, it's an unanswered question that I know is going to gnaw at me from time to time. Maybe Alma or I will bump into someone in the neighborhood who knows the guy's story. Maybe not. I sigh, look out the window across the aisle at the passing tile-roofed buildings on one of Lisbon's hills: so many people there I'll never meet or, if I do, never understand. Always a rube, never one of the locals. Or maybe the alchemists had it right—they were indeed transforming outwardly unpromising substances into gold, but, like an earnest foreigner navigating another land, they were locked in a Zeno-ish process that always kept them an increasingly tiny half-step from the glittering prize.

BREAD, BREAD; CHEESE, CHEESE

I wake to the *szizz* of the apartment's buzzer. Someone must be standing outside the lobby door, trying to get in. It's early, and one glance at Alma's quiet outline under the covers tells me that she's at least an hour away from waking, so I hustle into jeans, a shirt, as the buzzer goes off again, and then again. Before I can make it to the door, there's knocking on our window—one of the side benefits of living in a ground-floor apartment, I suppose. Who is this? We don't know anyone well enough to occasion a morning visit unannounced, and—there's that knocking again—we certainly don't know anyone *rude*.

I glance out the window. It's the mailman, I think. I've never met him before, and though he's not wearing a uniform (one minus check), he is holding a stack of letters and bills, magazines and a package (one plus check), and he's standing outside the door to the apartment lobby, where the mailboxes are. He's speaking earnestly, but I can't make out a thing—ribbons and curls of dream still cling to and escape from me. He seems official enough, so I nod, walk to our door, and push the button that will let him in.

It doesn't seem to work. I can hear him still rattling that door outside but no go, the thing's still locked. I hurry down to the lobby's glass-walled entrance.

"Obrigado"—thank you—he says, as I hold open the door, and then he unfurls a Portuguese wordscape that speeds by with only one little landmark that I recognize: *tocar*, which means "to ring." Ah, he must be telling me that the buzzer connection for the lobby entrance doesn't seem to work, probably wants me to tell the manager, but I can't even squeak out "Eu sei"—I know—or "Eu compreéndo"—I understand—much less construct a proper sentence as I stand there, struck dumb. I even forget to introduce myself, because I'm in Other Language Freefall. It's the linguistic equivalent of a Wile E. Coyote moment, when, rushing headlong off your butte of choice, you stand in the sky and recognize your dilemma, just before the air reasserts its traditional relationship with gravity and you begin your long, swift journey to becoming a puff of dust on the ground below.

I've lived in extended Other Language Freefall before, in African villages, and then I had a decent excuse—Alma and I were living among a people who spoke a virtually unrecorded language, Beng. There were no books written about it to prepare us, no common words shared with English (and don't even get me started about how, in Beng, *pronouns* are conjugated), so we just had to jump in and hold on. But I've been studying Portuguese on and off for years. So when the mailman stares with growing curiosity at silent me, I blush with embarrassment and finally squeak out, "Fala divigar, faz favor"—Speak slowly, please—an idiotic request, because even if he speaks at the pace of paint peeling I'll be lost.

He smiles—mystery over. My words have placed me in the category of Foreigner Struggling with the Local Language, and he realizes he'll simply have to tell someone else about the broken buzzer. I'm off the hook.

Depressed and humiliated, but off the hook. Living in a country where you're still tackling the language adds particular small dramas to each day, where ordinary speech is a mysterious puzzle. Little moments like the Doorbell Incident are not meant to weaken one's resolve but to strengthen it, so I suck it up and, over breakfast (buttered and toasted dark bread from the Serra da Estrela and black tea from the island of São Miguel, in the Azores; I am nothing if not a completist in my admiration of Portuguese culture), I dig into the local paper, elbowing my way through sentences with a dictionary, if necessary. It's sometimes slow work, trying to decipher "O Caso Mateus"—a soccer scandal involving three lower-ranked teams fighting a nasty legal battle for a berth in the premier league—or following the reports of an alarming string of forest fires sweeping the Portuguese countryside.

Yes, slow work, because sometimes I take a break and search in the dictionary for intriguing idiomatic phrases, the kind of nuggets that'll sparkle up a sentence. The first to catch my eye (probably because it's the name of a restaurant down the road from us) is *dizer pão, pão, queijo, queijo*—to say bread is bread, cheese is cheese—which means to speak the truth, to pull no punches. Then I find *a galinha do vizinho é sempre mais gordo*—the neighbor's chicken is always fatter—which is the Portuguese way of saying "The grass is always greener..."

Ah, I'm on a roll. I take in the last sips of my tea and find *Ele não apita em nada em casa*, which roughly translates as "He doesn't have a say in anything at home." *Apitar* means "to whistle," and I suspect that this "whistle" isn't meant to be the common purse-your-lips-together kind but instead what a soccer referee blasts out when announcing a foul. But who would I ever dare say that out loud about? My favorite discovery is *cair das nuvens*—to fall from the clouds—a great way to describe being astounded.

All this mining of phrases is my way of warming up for the big game ahead: speaking actual sentences in actual conversations with actual Portuguese. I repeat the words, try out the sounds in my mouth, imagine speaking them and astounding friends and family. (But who am I kidding? I've never in my entire life said "The grass is always greener" in *English*.)

At the sound of these verbal pushups, Alma walks into the living room and smiles her I-love-your-weirdness smile. Alma's style is different, and probably better: she doesn't mind jabbering away in public, making tons of mistakes but somehow getting her point across. She learned this in the rough-and-tumble world of fieldwork, and she's great at it. I'm a worrywart of a writer who obsesses over the teeniest nuances of words when I write, so I have a horror of blurting out a doozy of a mistake.

Just like the mistake I commit later that afternoon when I greet our neighborhood grocer, newly returned from a short vacation. From my mouth escapes the beginnings of "Boa viagem" (Bon voyage) before I manage to switch in midgear to "Bem vindo" (Welcome back). Our kindly grocer shrugs off my embarrassment, but even my bones and the white corpuscles in my veins briefly blush red. I buy some potatoes and onions for dinner and then walk to a nearby park, where two windmills on a hill look down on gardens, a pond, winding walkways. I wouldn't mind a breather from my past few hours of noodling on a novel passage, so I sit on a shaded bench, close my eyes, and simply listen to the speech of people passing by. I love the sound of Portuguese, I really do—it's more than music to my ears. It's such an indefinably delicious sonic feast that I imagine I'm falling from the clouds.

But for all my infatuation with the language, I do have a complaint—oh, do I—the kind of complaint that insists on calling bread, bread.

The Portuguese swallow their syllables.

It's almost a national pastime. They can take a perfectly fine sentence and, when they speak, reduce it to a half or a third of its original length. When it comes to spoken Portuguese, what you don't hear is as important as what you do. *Estas certo!*—You're right—becomes *Sta cert!* A 50 percent linguistic reduction is impressive, but when *Eu estou*—I am—can be snipped to something that sounds like *tou*, we're talking a 75 percent drop in syllabic reality. I imagine that if the Portuguese dictionary were written as the language is truly spoken, the book would be the size of a pamphlet listing the late-blooming flowers of North African mountaintops. I'd bet the barn that if Abraham Lincoln had been Portuguese, he could have delivered the 286 words of the Gettysburg Address in about twelve seconds.

I sit under this tree in a well-manicured corner of the park and work myself up into a particularly despairing and mean-spirited mood about my linguistic progress, so when I hear the keening of a distant ambulance, I imagine that paramedics are rushing to the hospital some poor gasping Portuguese soul who swallowed too many syllables at one time. There must be, after all, a magic cutoff point where, if you go too far, you choke on one final indigestible syllable. I wouldn't be surprised if each hospital here in Lisbon has a special Phonetic Reclamation Unit, with the best units boasting a gleaming, state-of-the-art syllable pump that draws out with gentle care from failing patients the severed sounds of too many words, phrases, sentences.

Maybe when Portuguese gather in small crowds on street corners and chat away, they're taking part in a secret competition where every conversation is actually a dangerous game—skirting right up to the edge of the syllable that might do you in, but not crossing the line. Challenging each other's syllable-subtraction prowess, they admire hearing a sentence gulped down to its basic components, they salute the best devil-may-care ingesting of a word's rightful sounds.

I walk back to the apartment, along streets that must be littered with the ghosts of syllables left unspoken, an invisible cemetery of the latest Portuguese parts of speech fallen in battle.

✳

After dinner, Alma, Hannah, and I stroll to a free open-air concert of fado music. It's billed as a pairing of Carlos do Carmo, one of the grand old figures of fado, and a younger singer I'm not familiar with, Camané, with a small orchestra. What I'm really excited about is that Ricardo Rocha will accompany each singer on Portuguese guitar. Rocha is the Ornette Coleman of the instrument, drawing out odd harmonies and creating aptly unexpected solos, and he should certainly keep the evening more than interesting.

A temporary stage has been set up before a vast lawn beside the Torre de Belém—the great fifteenth-century architectural monument perched in the shallows of the Tejo River (and when, by the way, did as musical a word as Tejo get translated into the ugly English oom-pah-pah of "Tagus"?). The tower is lit up against a clear sky and a hefty fraction of rising moon. Alma, Hannah, and I manage to find ourselves a place in the huge, standing-room-only crowd spread across the lawn, and the fact that this lawn is also dotted here and there with huge inflated rubber Sagres beer cans is something I allow myself to ignore.

When Carlos do Carmo walks onstage, a family standing beside us murmurs among themselves what sounds like concern for his health, and if I'm hearing correctly it's not surprising—he looks frail, even from a distance, and his voice, as he begins by reciting a poem about Lisbon, is hesitant, hoarse. I wonder if he can possibly sing, but I'm also on his side—he's speaking so slowly I feel a rush of gratitude that I can understand almost every word.

He falters a bit in the first song but somehow regains form by the second, and while Ricardo Rocha churns out his inventive, spidery filigrees, Carlos takes ever more confident turns with the smoother, more polished Camané. By the time the orchestra settles onstage for the final part of the concert, the white-haired master could almost be a young man again, if you closed your eyes.

Camané exits, leaving the stage to Carlos, whose repertoire includes "Canoas do Tejo" (Canoes on the Tejo River) and "Lisboa menina e moça" (Lisbon Girl and Maiden). I can make out only about a third of the lyrics, but one thing is certainly clear, as Alma jokes: *lisboetas* have a nearly bottomless pit of songs celebrating their city. That's all right by me; I love the place, too (especially its literate soul: questions about poets and novelists are regular features on TV quiz shows, and collectible coins featuring José Saramago and Fernando Pessoa come free with the morning newspaper; in America, it's cause for celebration if the president can bring himself to parse a simple sentence).

By now the audience is singing along, misty-eyed at tunes they clearly grew up with. Carlos catches the mood and stops before his last song to thank us all for coming, to thank the organizers of this *espectáculo*.

Except that he says "spec-tac-ul," which I count as a drop not of five syllables to three but of five to two and a half—or maybe even to just two, since that *ul* at the end barely makes it past his lips. For a moment I wait for him to clutch his throat and stagger across the stage as that *ul* parks itself in his esophagus. But no, he bestows a few more thanks, the violinists in the orchestra raise their bows, and Carlos do Carmo belts out the last song of the evening.

As we return home, following along with the happy, *saudade*-besotted crowd, I decide that I don't care if the Portuguese aren't hooked on phonics. That half-gulped *ul*, after all, was kind of cool. So if I'm calling bread, bread, then I should also call cheese, cheese. Maybe my neighbors are so fond of the lovely particular notes of their musical language—the *ooshes* and *oishes* and *aows*—that they clip as many intervening syllables as possible in order to get to each *oosh* faster. It's actually all this confounded swallowing that creates the wave of sound I love, the words melting their discrete borders into a collective enterprise that rises and falls together, like the houses dotting the hills of Lisbon.

Let's Throw a Festival!

We're tucking into our meals with real gusto in this restaurant over-looking the Tejo River, trying to finish before a fireworks display begins at the nearby marina of the Parque das Nações. In two days Hannah will start sixth grade at a Portuguese public school that's a few minutes' walk from our apartment, and Alma and I want to give her a booming sendoff and add a celebratory air to a big step that we're all nervous about. Hannah has long hoped for her own adventure (to match the months Nathaniel, now in college, spent living in an African village with us before she was born), and though Lisbon is far from the dangers and raucous joy of life in a small African village, it's nothing to sniff at. Hannah will soon be trying to pass tests and make new friends, all in a new language, and maybe dealing with the risks of contracting malaria or of encountering snakes and scorpions would be less challenging.

So, eyes on the clock, we scarf down our food. Usually I love the pace of Portuguese dining, with food a leisurely punctuation to good conversation. But Alma and I are already calculating that we'll pass up dessert so we won't miss the excitement, because tonight will be no ordinary popping of firecrackers: it's the second Saturday of the Mundial de Pirotecnia, Lisbon's international fireworks festival. Last week the Italians showed off their stuff; tonight it's the Germans' turn. On the following Saturday nights, the United States and then Portugal will get their chance to sizzle a decent expanse of sky. Everyone in the world, it seems, loves to blow up stuff to celebrate something, and for this festival, the fireworks experts get a chance to simply celebrate themselves.

While Alma promises Hannah we'll stop at a *pastelaria* later on the way home, I search for a glimpse of our waiter. As far as I can tell, the fellow must be off in some other busy corner, because he's certainly not hiding in the shadows—the lighting is chain-restaurant bright. (The "traditional" Portuguese cuisine in this place has an Olive Gardenish assembly-line taste.) We gotta get that check—the fireworks should be starting any minute, and while I scan the room again for our seemingly invisible waiter, I wonder what the peaceful contemporary nation of Germany is up to these days when it comes to big bangs. Thanks to the Portuguese love of festivals of all kinds, we're going to find out soon.

That's the Portuguese for you—they can turn anything into a festival, and they stretch bunches of them across every month of the calendar. This month a *commedia dell'arte* festival overlaps with a Shostakovich music festival, which competes with a festival of contemporary Chinese music, not to mention the Lisboa Dança festival, the Festival de Cinema Gay e Lésbico de Lisboa, and a Festival de Flamenco. These are followed by the Luzboa public-art festival. Already on next month's horizon a festival of live music approaches, alongside the documentary film festival Doclisboa and the Festival "Temps d'Images." Farther down the line, preparations are being made for electronic music, digital art, and African film festivals.

They're the secular equivalent of the country's religious calendar, with its panoply of saint's days and holidays as regular as stages of the cross. It's hard to escape Lisbon's festival mania, even if you're minding your own business with no ticket in hand. One evening, while Alma, Hannah, and I were strolling through the Chiado district, we turned a corner and came upon a band participating in a Dixieland music festival. They were setting up just outside the Café a Brasileira, dressed in white shirts and pants with red suspenders and toting the requisite trumpets, clarinet, trombone, and stripped-down drum kit. They spoke Spanish among themselves—not, I thought, a good sign. But when they ripped into "Sweet Georgia Brown" it was clear they'd done the necessary homework on New Orleans–style jazz.

There's a particular Portuguese genius to all these festivals. If you can't go to all the events, you at least know that other aspects of, say, flamenco dancing, or new Chinese music, are being covered elsewhere, thank you very much. A single concert or performance simply can't exhaust a subject—it's just one color of the art form's full spectrum. I'm sure Fernando Pessoa, who invented multiple poets within him in order to express his full artistic range, would heartily agree.

Now we can hear the first telltale distant booms through the glass wall beside our table, and we can just make out, through the reflection of the restaurant behind us, the first soaring patterns in the sky outside. Finally I catch the waiter's eye, and when he returns with the *conta*, I leave a bigger tip than usual because I don't want to wait for the change. It's too late now to run down to the marina, so instead we settle for the wooden deck surrounding the restaurant, and we lean on the railing, our heads raised to the ruckus above. Flaring red spirals coil and hiss in the sky, staggered multiple discharges overlap, and a circle of green tracers expands like an exhalation of breath, until the boom kicks in. There's always that delay between the inventive flash and the roar that set it off, because light travels to the eye faster than sound travels to the ear. It's a little like the delay between the punch line and the laugh, and part of the pleasure of fireworks, I realize, is anticipating what any particularly robust, flaring design will eventually sound like.

As the flashy hubbub continues, Hannah leans tentatively, first against me, then Alma—unusual, since she's the type of child who will whirl down a hallway with a cartwheel or burst into her latest favorite song with no warning. At eleven, she's young enough to still be impressed by tonight's display but old enough to think that she's, well, too old for it all, though I suspect that the approach of this Monday's first day of school is what really has her distracted. Alma has a faraway look in her eyes, too, and probably for the same reason. For the past week or so, my wife has been in Full Mother Jacket—at the local *papelaria* she ordered Hannah's schoolbooks and supplies for the year, and she even managed to locate another girl in the school who speaks English. Meanwhile, I've been doing my best to keep Hannah's spirits up with my goofy jokes and shenanigans, and with my bright ideas like taking in tonight's slice of a fireworks festival. We're a family, after all, in for this year's adventure together.

Soon enough we warm to the busy doings above and relax enough to release our obligatory *ooob*s and *aaab*s at shivering white centers of filigree that crackle like enormous sparklers in the sky. Though I don't see what's particularly Germanic about these spectacular flourishes, I find myself filled with memories of other displays, from my own personal fireworks festival. When I was much younger and (only slightly) stupider, I stood on a wooden bridge in a small town in Japan and watched bursts of cranes and flower blossoms explode out of the darkness for the Bon Odori celebration. Another time, Alma and I stood at the railing of a friend's rented boat in the East River and watched fireworks celebrating the one-hundredth anniversary of the Brooklyn Bridge, an extraordinary fanfare that was mirrored by the river and by the glass windows of Lower Manhattan's office buildings and skyscrapers, including the World Trade Center. That image—of festive explosions rippling across the sides of the Twin Towers—haunted me years later, when I did volunteer work near Ground Zero.

So while tonight's sky is impressively frisky, there's this other reason that I'm still lagging behind in the enjoyment department: last week was the fifth anniversary of 9/11. On the day, the three of us took a bus across the Tejo River to the town of Setúbal, to catch a boat that offered dolphin watching in the local freshwater inlets. But we just missed the cutoff and were left to stand on the dock and watch the sailboat glide off into the bay. Only then did I realize how much I'd wanted to be distracted by the frolics of Flipper's Portuguese cousins. I should have remembered that there's no running away from what you can't forget.

These hearty booms and streams of burning sky are not only a metaphor for joy and celebration; they remind me of real-world explosions with real-world consequences, and I think of a novel I've been reading, *Sleepwalking Land* by Mia Couto, a writer from the former Portuguese colony of Mozambique. It's a hallucinatory look at the ravaged landscape of Mozambique's civil war, with often harrowing images balanced by the poetic grace of the prose. Every few pages I've had to take out my notebook and copy down another sentence I simply couldn't let escape through the porous cheesecloth of my memory. One line that's wrapped itself around my brain is that each of us is a "sleepwalker strolling through fire." Uh-huh—I've collected enough psychic burns of varying degrees and of my own making to say amen to that, brother. But there's another quote I've collected that comes back to me now, one so apt that I wonder if it led me, unconsciously, to suggest, days ago, that we all take in some fireworks: "They should invent a gentle, more affable gunpowder, capable of exploding men without killing them. An inverse powder, which would generate more life. And out of one exploded man, the infinity of men inside him would be born." Now wouldn't *that* be a great addition to a fireworks festival, a thrilling new pyrotechnic tradition. And what a welcome innovation it would be in the art of war.

Fat chance.

So we'll certainly be passing on next week's entry in the festival, the United States—we've had enough of our country's Shock and Awe and its ilk to last us a lifetime. (And I can't say that Alma, given her Jewish heritage, has been entirely thrilled that this evening's explosions are brought to us by Germany.) On the other hand, I might not have worked myself up like this if these fireworks tonight had been their own singular event instead of an entry in a multinational festival. The Portuguese get it right—there's more bang for your buck when a single performance doesn't pretend to be the last word. Everything can change—"depende do contexto," as our language tutor often says.

Finally, the night sky reclaims its darkness, its silence, and the crowd begins to disperse. Alma, Hannah, and I hold each other's hand and set off for our delayed dessert at the closest *pastelaria* we can find. There, we return to our own particular context: a family in a foreign country, sweetening our awareness of this year's uncertainties with a *pastel de nata* or a *bola de chocolate*, the swoosh and burst of skyrockets still ringing in our ears.

ISN'T THERE A LAW AGAINST FILCHING A CALÇADA?

Give me a spare hour or so in the evening and I'll gladly spend it wandering up and down the hills of Lisbon, letting the fictional characters inside me have a chance to jostle among themselves while I'm drawn to the sight of a *tasca* with chickens and rabbits hanging in the window, or the elaborately sculpted facade of a tucked-away church, or a bar where all eyes are trained on a small screen's soccer drama. Just as often, though, my eyes are down, attentive to the art beneath my feet: the cobblestones of Lisbon.

Unlike the eternal unrolling of concrete carpet you'll find in any American city or town, there's nowhere in Lisbon where you can avoid the sight of stone-cobbled streets or sidewalks. And why would anyone want to, since these alternating white and black limestone cobbles—*calçadas*—ripple inventively down the sidewalk in wavelike or checkerboard patterns, or as designs of flower petals, rays of light, interlocking chain links, even depictions of caravels with a crow in what I guess must be the crow's-nest. This entire idea of walking on art has a direct ancestry to the tiled floor decorations of Roman villas back when Portugal was a western province of the empire. In a culture so steeped in the mournful nostalgia of *saudade*, I suppose it makes sense that nearly every pathway in Lisbon would echo the past.

Yet tonight, as I stand here on a corner facing the Museu Nacional de Etnologia, I'm impressed by its broad sidewalks of *calçadas* not because of their designs—they don't have 'em—but because there are just so *many* of them, thousands upon thousands, a field of white stones stretching off into the distance. So many that I can't help wondering, how many *are* there?

It'd certainly be a long, long haul if I tried to count each one. Impossible. Yet the idea tugs at me—couldn't there be an easier way? Math for me is a vestigial organ—aside from counting out change at the store, and as long as the page numbers of any book I'm reading remain consecutive, the subject doesn't cross my mind. But I'm sure that I can remember enough of the stuff from the Paleolithic of my childhood to give multiplication a try. So first I count a single line of stones across the width of the wide sidewalk, from inner border to curb: forty-six. Damn, fifty would be better, considering my math skills, but I resist the impulse to round off—this is serious business, and I want to be as accurate as possible.

Now it's time for the next step. The curb itself is bordered along its length by a series of narrow cement tiles. I measure the length of three or four and discover that, on average, each tile is about eight cobblestones long. I take out the notebook I carry with me everywhere, which I like to think of as my little portable idol, my rented golem ("Ídolo portátil / O livro é / um golem alugado," as the Portuguese poet Ana Hatherly writes). Pen in hand and revving up my ancient computational synaptic connections, I multiply 46 by 8 and come up with 368 stones.

Ah, but my task has just begun. Next, I have to walk down the length of the sidewalk, to count the number of cement border tiles. I balance on the edge of the curb, arms out, feeling like a kid again, and set off, counting one, two, three, four, and I've got a long way to go; the end of the block seems far, far away—28, 29, 30—and though the street is deserted, what would I do if someone turned a corner and saw me—52, 53, 54—counting out loud in English (easier to remember that way), as if self-administering a Breathalyzer test?

I stop. Was that 67 or 68? Damn, I have to concentrate. I decide to play it safe and say 67, and walk on, slower now. No funny stuff, simply pay attention to this weighty matter at hand, but the Tejo River is in view and I love how the moonlight shimmers on its surface. After a couple more rough spots of concentration, I've balanced my way to the end, to the reward of knowing that the block is 135 border tiles long.

Now for the moment of truth. I multiply 135 by 368 and arrive at the daunting number of 49,680. Because there are four sides of sidewalk surrounding this museum, I then multiply this mouthful of a number (oh, I am on a roll) yet another time, now times 4, and this delivers unto me a grand total of 198,720 stones. That's not even counting all the cobbled courtyards dotting the museum grounds or the cobbled paths that connect to them and the parking lot—totaling those could jump it up to nearly a half-million!

Unaccustomed to so much counting, I'm feeling a little drunk with math, crazy enough to dare to guess how many stones there might be in the entire city of Lisbon: all those plazas large and small, and all the sidewalks, and all the streets and avenues. If merely two square blocks could add up to a million stones, and if a thousand million is a billion, then . . .

I'm not sure if it's possible, but another part of me says *Go on, give it a try*. So I bravely crunch some serious numbers in my notebook and come up with the roughly scientific estimation of a zillion gazillion. Even if my calculations are off by several gazillion, that would still be a lot. Our galaxy is made up of more than 100 billion stars—how would all the stones of Lisbon stack up to that?

Once again I regard the museum grounds, its multitude of stones. My work here is done. So I continue on my evening ramble, past a line of shops, a botanical garden, then circle back past one of the smaller soccer stadiums in the city, huff up a hill, and turn a corner where a portion of the sidewalk has been broken apart by a work crew earlier in the day. Feeling a bit proprietary about these stones (after all, I am the Calçada Counter), I kneel down for a closer look. The white ones are as often as not cream colored, while some have hints of gray, blue, or pink. There's nothing factory-made about them—each one is a little "off." Then I pick up one of the loose stones, and its essential cubicity weighs in. I twist and turn it in my hand and feel the attentive craft, how each of the stone's six sides has been carefully chipped to a rough approximation of a smooth surface. That must be why I feel such affection for these stones—they're as individual as people. But it's an affection laced with sadness, because so much of their originality—their five other sides—is normally buried out of sight. And that's a lot like people, too.

Each one radiates so much personality that I regret having numbered them—they deserve names instead. But in Portugal, unfortunately, you can bestow names only from an approved list administered by the Direcção-Geral dos Registos e Notariado. That must be the reason there are so many Joãos, Marias, and Josés coming out of the woodwork. Just the other day, though, I read in the newspaper that eighteen new first names have been approved by the Portuguese naming czars, newcomers with a little spice and verve, like Gildásio, Umbelina, Miqueias. This is more like it—who'd want a street full of stones named João João João João João João?

So what would I call this cobblestone in my hand? Probably not Atila, which is another of the recently approved names. Maybe Miqueias, because I'm guessing that for the rest of my life I'll never know how to pronounce this name properly, and a too-solid stone could use a little mystery.

Now that I've given it a name, how can I return it to the exposed, broken ground? And I *could* use a paperweight for my desk. I resume my stroll with little Miqueias, though when a couple cars pass by I cup the stone against my side, trying to hide the thing from the sight of the drivers. *Thief*, I think—isn't there a law against filching a *calçada*? I'm really only borrowing it, I fully intend to return it to the street before I leave the country, but then the voice of Miss Smith, my scary third-grade teacher (the one with the paddle and the pipe cleaners) intrudes from out of nowhere, and she's insisting, *That's no excuse—if everyone did this there wouldn't be any streets in Lisbon!*

Well, I reply (and I've been wanting to tell this woman off for decades), *apparently you haven't been paying attention, Miss Smith, or else you'd know that earlier this evening I established that there are far more stones in Lisbon than there are people in the world, in fact—*

A dog howls, and I almost leap out of my guilty skin. A quick glance at the snarling creature behind the fence and I realize that I'm walking along a street lined with embassies, each gated and likely protected by many more ready-to-bark-at-a-moment's-notice dogs. Perhaps not the best route to be taking while holding in my hand a nice-sized, potentially throwable stone. I imagine the security cameras of every house pulling in for a close-up of my right hand, calculating, on hidden digital screens, when I might rear back and hurl this stone through the tempting target of a wide-paneled window. So I grip the *calçada* tightly, as if I could somehow squeeze it out of sight, and hurry off.

A block or so away I slow down and relax and realize that the variations of little Miqueias's surfaces have made me attentive to the same sort of variations beneath my feet. Because each step I take feels different—the sidewalk's terrain is always slightly shifting, a new span of individually shaped stones supporting each stride. Maybe this is one of the reasons I've been enjoying these evening strolls so much: my feet are secretly hungry to read the streets' complex topographies. It's a kind of Braille that speaks of all the craftsmen over the centuries who broke large limestone blocks and tapped and shaped them into small cubes; of all the workers who placed line after line of them in the ground; and of who knows how many feet that daily step on this city's vast stretches of cobbled sidewalks.

I laugh, flip Miqueias in the air a couple of times, and keep walking. Given the chance, I could walk all night.

THE MOON, COME TO EARTH

I'm ready to hit the road, but my daughter has planted herself out-side our apartment, snapping photos of the night clouds that, mo-ment by moment, clip across the sky, obscuring and revealing the moon. A patient soul, Hannah holds the camera with care, in search of some elusively ideal moon-cloud ratio that I can only guess at. Last month, at a beach in Estoril, she tried to frame the full-winged flight of a seagull with the camera, and kept at it for over an hour until she got what she wanted. We don't have that kind of time now, so I gulp down a hefty dollop of guilt,

father (noun): the impatient, insensitive, callous, beetle-browed, knuckle-dragging male parent of a child

and pry my daughter from her latest challenge.

I have a good reason, I keep telling myself as Hannah and I hurry down the cobbled sidewalk. Ahead of us tonight lies a four-kilome-ter course up and down the hills of Lisbon, where selected streets and plazas have been transformed by a series of public art installa-tions exploring the medium of light. The whole caboodle has been wrapped up as a festival called Luzboa. Since Alma is out of town at a conference, I thought that Hannah would enjoy this little adven-ture (especially since tonight she has 100 percent dibs on the cam-era). A bit of entertainment is certainly in order, now that her sec-ond week of sixth grade is behind her. The Portuguese, at least in her school, seem to have a pedagogical tradition that's perhaps best described as I Speak, You Listen. *And* listen in Portuguese, which she's only beginning to learn. I can't help thinking of now college-ensconced Nathaniel, who lived in a small African village with Alma and me when he was six, because at first he didn't speak a word of the local language either. He was a great whistler, though, and with a combination of birdlike trills and hand gestures he shed his usual shyness—soon he was running along the paths and through the odd corners of the village with a crowd of new friends.

Hannah and I flag down a cab and before long we arrive at the Praça Príncipe Real, a small park that marks the beginning of the festival's walk. I love this *praça* because of its monumental cedar tree, whose lower branches, supported from below by an elaborate iron grillwork, fan out in an almost impossibly wide circle, a vast umbrella of green shade. A truly awe-inspiring sight, but at night the darkness claims it, so we wander about the park until we find the first installation. Titled *Coraçao*—Heart—it's a branching network of thin red neon tubes that resembles a huge, radioactive spider's web, and it hovers just above the ground, making a rough, wide circle around a small tree. The whole contraption shivers slightly in the breeze, and when Hannah leans in for a closer look, she points out the nearly transparent plastic wires holding the various stresses together.

This delicate artwork, I realize, is a deliberate echo of the grillwork supporting the famous cedar tree on the other side of the park. It also suffers by comparison—some things really shouldn't be trifled with. So we continue along the festival's course down a sloping hill, guided by the colored lights of selected street lamps. The next few installations don't have nearly the zip we'd hoped for, and off my mind goes again, back to Africa and Nathaniel, and how—his whistle language established—he and his village pals commandeered a pile of old discarded mud bricks and managed to assemble marvelous, winding fortlike structures, decorating them with blushes of bright red flowers that blossomed on nearby trees. Even though each night the village goats would scale those walls and knock them—

Hannah pulls at my sleeve and gives me The Look, a mixture of exasperation and mystified indulgence that's become a family staple whenever it's clear that my mind has skipped town for a beat or two,

father (noun): the airy-headed, self-absorbed, anxious, and distracted reverie-monger male parent of a child

or three, or four, or more.

"Dad, *look*," she's saying, and I stop and stare. We've come upon a Ben & Jerry's, of all places. We are instantly its latest customers. After choosing a cone stacked with chocolate, Hannah insists that we sit in a corner, away from the crowd, and for her I guess this minor anonymity hits the spot as much as the ice cream does. Shyness has always been an alien concept for my daughter, but her role as a *norteamericana* object of intense curiosity in her school must surely be tiring. So I can't help myself—I wind up my mantra that this year will end up being an extraordinary experience for her, and Hannah can only stare at me: as far as she's concerned, the jury's still out on Portugal. I shut up and enjoy the ice cream, though I can't help silently wishing that my daughter's task were as easy as catching a bird on the wing or a cloud across the moon.

Despite the unexpected windfall of American-style ice cream, our evening has been long on walking, short on inspiration. Still, we continue down the hill into the Chiado neighborhood, in search of the festival's next installation. A turn here, a turn there, and we find a huge sphere, like a moon, sitting in the corner of a recessed plaza, made of some sort of durable white canvas; it's lit from within like a giant light bulb, and across its surface are painted stretches of lunar craters and mountain ranges. More than a few of the people passing by stage goofy poses before it, casting themselves as temporary stars in their own remake of *E.T.*

Perking up, Hannah murmurs, "So pretty." The moon, it appears, has come to earth tonight, magically, just for her, and even if it has left the shifting clouds behind, Hannah radiates concentration and lines up her shots. I decide to give her all the time she needs, suspecting that my daughter must feel some kinship with this fallen moon. After all, they're fellow travelers, taken out of context and isolated. I lean back on a stone bench and marvel at just how private public art can be.

Alma and I have always dragged our children along with us over hill and dale, a family ethos we've never really thought to question, but tonight, watching Hannah take tentative steps toward the moon for a close-up of the craters and ridges, I can't help doubting myself. She takes one last photo. "Goodbye," she says wistfully. Then Hannah turns and half smiles at me across the plaza, a sad and dreamy expression that almost breaks my heart. With a step, my daughter pulls away from her moon, and if I were a better father, this would be a perfect moment to call it quits and return to the apartment,

father (noun): the selfish, willful, take-care-of-number-one, oblivious, and utterly clueless male parent of a child

but a devil named We're Not Finished Yet has claimed my soul.

Soon enough we arrive at the base of the hills and winding streets of the Alfama, Lisbon's old Moorish quarter. After climbing a series of steep, narrow steps, Hannah and I are greeted by *Fado Morgano*: a series of banners hanging above us in the air, lit from various angles and each filled with a color photo of a face—men and women, young and old, eyes closed. A haunting recorded chant seems to seep out of the walls of the alley. I'm struck by the eerie beauty of this disembodied crowd. Hannah sits on the steps in a corner, hunched over, and I'm shocked. My daughter is a truly social creature who usually loves anything to do with people, yet these floating faces have seriously creeped her out. She must feel as if she's back in the classroom, surrounded by schoolmates she still doesn't know how to reach. While it's true that I can walk in a distracted haze, that I can ignore what's right in front of me, that I'm oblivious and willful and impatient, it's also true that sometimes I *can* catch a clue. It's time to cut short our little art tour.

✳

A week later, Alma, Hannah, and I squeeze together in the backseat of a cab and set off for home after a lively dinner at the apartment of the writer Gonçalo Tavares and the artist Rachel Caiano. Hannah's tuckered out from all the energy of their three young children, but by the time the taxi is skirting along the edge of the Tejo River she somehow rouses herself and starts listing the names of her classmates. This is Classic Hannah, who has always, ever since she was able to talk, loved naming dolls, stuffed animals, even anonymous characters in picture books. (I'd sometimes dread turning a page to a crowd scene, because she'd spend as long as it took to bestow a name upon each of the hundreds of tiny figures before we could continue with the story.) So now Alma and I are listening to her latest list, featuring Sandro and João, Catarina and Dário, José and Ana-Beatrize, Filipa and Sara, each name with its own slippery landscape of Portuguese pronunciation. I've never quite noticed it before, but already Hannah has that soft raspy roll of the Portuguese *rrrrrr* down perfectly, as well as the round plummy richness of some of the vowels.

"Now you try," Hannah says.

I smile ruefully and give it a go, knowing that my stumbling will fuel my daughter's self-confidence, will inflate her water wings in this sea of a new language we've thrown her into. She's a tough taskmaster, and Alma and I glance at each other over her head, trying to tamp down our delighted relief at our daughter's new authority as she chastens us for our hopeless accents. We try our best to pronounce the words correctly, oh we do try, but our mouths have spent too many decades shaping themselves around the contours of English. Hannah's voice, however, trips lightly over every nuance. The language's entire vocabulary patiently awaits her.

As we near our apartment, I lean forward in the back seat and trot out my ritual final directions, but when I stumble over *em frente*—straight ahead—Hannah corrects me, clipping the syllables just right. Then she takes over and gives the rest of the directions, in beautifully inflected Portuguese, to the cab driver, who's been listening silently to our backseat language lesson the whole ride. "Sim, Professora," he chuckles, and with a turn here, a turn there, he gets us all—proud parents, playfully imperious daughter—back home just fine.

THOSE TRICKY SUBGESTURES

I step out of the cab and pay the driver, adding a modest tip that's still larger than anything anyone else in Lisbon would ever give. Usually I wouldn't dream of bucking local custom, but in this case I don't care—as a college student, I spent one summer driving a cab in New York City, and I haven't forgotten how tough the job can be.

I stand at the corner, glancing left and right. My friend Rui Zink is late—or should I, as an American living in Portugal, say that I'm early? Lately I've been hanging out with Rui, a fine writer who can work in any genre imaginable. A gregarious, opinionated, generous fellow, Rui seems to get invited to everything, and sometimes he'll give me a call if he thinks I might be interested. Tonight I'm *very* interested: the Nobel laureate José Saramago, in town for the week, is attending the launching of a book of essays about his work.

I'm psyched. In Saramago's novels the Iberian Peninsula can break off from Europe and float free in the Atlantic Ocean, or a plague of blindness will unravel the inner and outer worlds of its victims. In *The Year of the Death of Ricardo Reis*, Reis, one of the poet Fernando Pessoa's invented alter egos, survives his creator's death and wanders through the streets of Lisbon. I read that book with a map by my side, a year before my first trip to Lisbon; it's how I first began to learn my way around the city. And Saramago's prose! It's surprisingly, entertainingly readable, considering that it inhabits a time all its own: either some prepunctuation Paleolithic of the sentence or a postapocalyptic grammatical future where a literary neutron bomb has wiped most periods and quotation marks from the face of the earth. It's a kind of magic, to be able to write fiction that *looks* so difficult and yet isn't.

The cultural foundation sponsoring tonight's do is somewhere on this block, so I continue down the street, approaching four guards who stand before an official-looking building, two of them sporting machine guns. They certainly have down pat that air of casual menace so popular among the machine-gun-toting masses, and because I'm walking with a bag big enough to contain any number of suspicious items (one of Saramago's novels, my notebook, a camera), I look straight ahead, trying to exude an air of *I'm going about my own peaceful business, no need to worry about me.*

A couple of motorcycles rush by, leading the way for a few very official-looking cars, their lights flashing. I'm guessing it's not considered polite to stare, so I feign disinterest and concentrate on my search for the foundation. After wandering up and down the street a couple times, I notice a tiny brass plaque beside a heavy wooden door. This must be the place, but Rui is the one with the invitation, so I walk across the street and wait.

Folks are starting to arrive now, entering through the door. Still no sign of Rui. I think of calling him but hesitate. The guards down the street aren't that far away, and if they saw me punching numbers into a phone . . . Haven't cell phones been used by terrorists to set off explosions? I hope those guards don't have trigger fingers. Then I laugh, because I can't believe I'm still giving in to this War on Terror paranoia—especially since the Republicans' asses were so soundly and justly handed to them in the recent midterm elections, and on a silver platter—

There's Rui, marching up the street. He's in the shadows, but I know him by his walk. Rui is a bear of a guy, almost anti-Portuguese in body size, and he has a bit of a limp. He's embarrassed to admit it (and also eager to admit it, Rui is like that), but he forgot where the street was and got lost. Well, *não faz mal*—no harm done—because, hey, just look at me: my body's completely unriddled with bullets! We enter the building, have our names ticked off a list, then march down a surprisingly large number of stairways to the lecture hall.

At once I locate a short line of people waiting for Saramago to sign books. His face is an odd mixture of severity and calm, with the occasional wan smile softening it all. He looks approachable, and part of me would really like to have him sign my copy of *Ricardo Reis*. But when it comes right down to it, I know I'm not going to snag a signature or snap a photo. Either souvenir, I realize, would be irrelevant to the impact his books have had on me. That brain encased in his skull is what I'm here for, the one that has already generated some of my favorite novels. I hope at least a few more are fermenting in there.

Eventually, everyone starts to settle into seats, and I can see that we're in for an evening of speeches, because an international mix of four scholars—two Portuguese, a Brazilian, an Englishman—have lined up in a row on the small stage.

They look terrified.

Why shouldn't they be? Saramago is right there before them, sitting in the front row! Imagine presenting some cobbled-together lit crit in front of, say, a reincarnated James Joyce or Leo Tolstoy, come back from the dead to be entertained for an evening.

The Portuguese start with the first two presentations. These days, I'm good for understanding about 10 percent of spoken Portuguese. The stone of the language skips across the surface of my understanding, the curve of its trajectory giving me at least the gist of what's being said. Catching visual cues helps, too, and what I'm noticing is that the Portuguese scholars sit a little too stiffly, their body language a picture-perfect model of the advanced stages of calcification. When it's finally the Brazilian scholar's turn to speak, however, she quickly sheds her nervousness and teases Saramago, looks directly at him and thanks him for everything he's written, and she even calls her fellow panelists *nossa equipa*—our team—as if they're a bunch of literary midfielders, kicking a Saramago soccer ball back and forth. She can't suppress a little samba sway as she speaks.

So far, everyone seems to be conforming to cultural stereotypes, yet this must be too easy an observation, one that ignores a whole range of subtleties beyond my ken. I can't help thinking of one of my favorite passages in all of Saramago's work, a sentence from his novel *The Double* that I've often quoted and discussed with my students: "People say, for example, that Tom, Dick or Harry, in a particular situation, made this, that or the other gesture, that's what we say, quite simply, as if the this, that or the other, a gesture expressing doubt, solidarity or warning were all of a piece, doubt always prudent, support always unconditional, warning always disinterested, when the whole truth, if we're really interested, if we're not to content ourselves with only the banner headlines of communication, demands that we pay attention to the multiple scintillations of the subgestures that follow behind a gesture like the cosmic dust in the tail of a comet, because, to use a comparison that can be grasped by all ages and intelligences, these subgestures are like the small print in a contract, difficult to decipher, but nonetheless there." Now this is a sentence whose winding ways are worth mulling over, but the English scholar has started speaking.

And he is one of my worst nightmares.

Clearly more nervous than the others, he lurches from sentence to sentence, his Portuguese accent sometimes on, sometimes off. Worse, he doesn't know when to quit. Maybe he's trying to prove he can redeem his initial faltering, but then he pauses, struggling to remember a word (oh, how many times have I done that!), and a few people in the audience offer, in a murmur, what they think he's looking for.

Rui can barely contain himself, but as for me, I feel this scholar's embarrassment as my own, having stumbled countless times in conversation. There's so much to remember in building a Portuguese sentence. Just this morning, while reading the newspaper, something about the use of the word *andar*—to walk—made me think it's not always used literally, so I opened up my sometimes too comprehensive Portuguese dictionary and almost cried at the sight of a long column of useful phrases designed to squeeze every last drop of metaphoric juice out of the word. One lousy verb, so many subgestures.

By this time, I'm staring at the floor. No way do I want to make eye contact, because, in truth, I can only aspire to this scholar's level of linguistic grief. I am a mere mote, a subatomic particle, an infinitesimal muon or quark, to the gas-giant planet of his shaky Portuguese. I can imagine him throwing up his hands in defeat, pointing at me, and saying to the audience, "Hey, you think *I'm* bad—why don't you try listening to *that* guy speak?"

After the poor fellow finally sputters out, he sits there, pinned to his chair, sporting a blush that's going for the world's record for blushing, and in two categories—depth of shade and duration. He may even sport traces of it when he has grandchildren, a tiny pink hint about his cheekbones that his family will whisper about.

Saramago is invited to join the panel onstage, and he accepts. He sits among them, calm, urbane, amused by it all, clearly satisfied with his portion of praise for the evening. He plays the part of a celebrated writer, gracious at the minor honor of this short stop on his long career, and begins a little impromptu speech. Hoping to catch some of what he's saying (why didn't I bring a tape recorder?), I silently will my ears to stretch out to Dumbo size, and I manage to suss out one tidbit: "All one needs to know in life," Saramago says, "is that others exist"; then he adds, "Life is not just 'me.'"

After a brief question-and-answer period, everyone is all talked out, and Rui insists on introducing me. He and Saramago have met before, and after a short chat Rui nods in my direction and describes me as an American writer living in Lisbon for the year. Saramago's face stiffens. He says to Rui, in icy Portuguese, "It's good that he came here, because I won't travel to his country, in protest."

I'm pretty sure I've heard correctly. Certainly it's clear that our little colloquy is over, so Rui and I make our way to the table where wine and *rissóis*—creamy shrimp turnovers—are being offered. Meanwhile, my mind starts up a great interior ruckus. What does Saramago think my citizenship makes me, anyway—a six-year smorgasbord of headlines featuring global warming, fundamentalist Christianity, illegal wiretapping, a war built on lies, legalized torture, that damn dog Barney? Hey, I voted against Bush twice, and I went through quite a rigmarole to mail my absentee ballot in time for the midterm elections, and then there's all the dough I sent to a whole gaggle of netroots Democratic candidates, and I used my Skype account on Election Day to make calls from Portugal for a get-out-the-vote effort, and—

I'm all revved up, but I keep it to myself. One of the lessons I've learned in life is that self-righteousness is best served as a private midnight snack. Still, wine glass in hand, I can't help asking Rui if I really did hear Saramago correctly. He'd rather not answer, but Rui is honest to a fault, and his quick, embarrassed grimace says it all. "Sometimes," he murmurs, "he's not the easiest person to get along with . . ."

Strangely enough, I feel an odd moment of affection for Saramago, who, after all, is just a fallible human being. It hasn't been all that rare in my life to encounter fellow writers who can crank up more compassion for their created characters than they can for the living, breathing souls around them. It's almost touching that tonight Saramago opted for headline rattling. It's so easy to miss the fine print.

After chatting with the writer Hélia Correia at the reception, congratulating her on a literary prize she has won for her latest novel, Rui and I head off for a late dinner at one of his favorite *tascas*. Our path down the street takes us right past those machine-gun guys, and I'm feeling a bit uneasy again, or, as the Portuguese say, *Eu ando com a pedra no sapato*, which literally means "I'm walking with a stone in my shoe."

"Who do you think they're protecting?" I wonder aloud, and Rui, ever curious and forthright, turns to ask the guards. They tell him it's the American ambassador's residence.

Yup, on closer look there's a small plaque by the front door, spelling it all out. There's an American flag flying from the third floor—how could I have first missed this, even if it's way up there? As for the ambassador, I've read a little about the guy—he's a longtime fundraiser for Bush and a businessman from Florida, of all states. I can't help thinking that he could have helped out in the stealing of the 2000 election (and for a moment I have this crazy image of him in a dimly lit room, gluing tiny chads back onto an election ballot). He's just the sort of right-winger I've fantasized standing in front of, red-faced, giving voice to the long list of all the curses I've ever learned, followed by a longer list of all their variations.

As Rui and I continue past the residence, I peer in at the impressively fenced-in grounds and notice something else I'd missed earlier in the evening. (I'm a writer, damn it—aren't I supposed to be alert to small details?) In the attached garden there's a play structure— swings, slide, little wooden tower—much like one I once built in my own backyard. Suddenly, I'm ashamed of the broad brush with which I've been painting. The ambassador must have small children, or at least grandchildren. His politics may set my teeth grinding, but now I can imagine him standing at a window, watching the kids outside swinging back and forth, or squealing down the slide, while a few feet away armed guards behind an iron fence protect them from the headlines of the world, headlines that as of yet they know nothing about.

Oh, those tricky subgestures.

NEARLY THE SAME SUBSTANCE

Our train speeds along, leaving behind first Lisbon and then its suburban sprawl. Soon we're in the countryside, which is dotted with field after flooded field, gifts of the terrible November rains: a month-long comprehensive anthology that studiously covered all major aspects of the subject, from Downpour and Showers through to Drizzle and Teasing Hint of Sun. But Downpour ruled the table of contents, and the rain fell so hard and so often that it felt personal as it abused umbrellas, sank shoes, and kindled a long-dormant appreciation for the invention of the roof.

The flooded fields alternate with little towns that often surround a small hill topped by a castle. The forbidding outlines of the ancient turrets and ramparts are a steady reminder into the present of past threats, past conflicts, though these days a healthy number of castles serve as *pousadas*—rather high-end hotels—that welcome invading tourists into the keep.

By now we're settled into the efficient comfort of the train's sleek interior, enjoying the prospect of the extended weekend before us. We could have stayed home, spent three days with our noses pressed against a window, watching rerun after rerun of the rain. But right now we're happy to get as far away as possible from Hannah's school, where it turned out that casual humiliation is a not insignificant daub of paint on the pedagogical palette, where some students indulge in chair flinging (practically a recognized school sport), where the largely unsupervised lunch breaks can stretch to nearly two *Lord of the Flies* hours, and where an inventive little bully has turned our daughter into a pet project. Hannah, so vulnerable with her still-budding Portuguese, has bravely tried to meet the challenge of this school, but Alma and I are convinced the challenge isn't worth winning.

Which is why next week Hannah switches to a new school, one where empathy and kindness reign. So this little trip is a kind of parenthesis, a farewell to two unhappy months at one school and a hopeful pause before the promise of the next. I look across at my daughter, who is deep in her latest preteen-populated novel, her head framed by the train window's passing scenes of flooded fields, and my relief at her escape is laced with guilt that she'll have to start from square one again.

Finally we arrive at Coimbra, a town that displays a venerable university instead of a castle perched on top of its hill. We haul our suitcases a few blocks from the station to our hotel, a long, thin building that tapers to a rounded end, like the prow of a ship. At least it feels like a ship's prow as we settle into our suite, because when I step out onto our front balcony, there's the dark Mondego River flowing slowly alongside us. On the street directly below, students loiter, dressed in their university's hundreds-of-years-old traditional fashion statement of Everything Black, even down to the impressive touch of long black capes—my God, these students aren't just bohemians, they're super bohemians. One holds a guitar, another a bass drum, and I remember reading that these kinds of troupes wander the streets of Coimbra, squeezing out as much street change as they can for their music. Students gotta eat.

Since I'm a little stir crazy after the train ride, I step back into the room and say, "C'mon, let's go outside, there's some concert about to start."

Alma doesn't stop emptying her suitcase, but she does give me a sidelong glance I know well, the one that means she's ready and willing to join any impromptu jaunt, just give her a minute.

"Hannah?" I call, but her room in this suite exudes silence. I don't have to walk in to know she's probably stretched across the bed with her book, still intent on the doings of fictional girls far away in America. She could use this spot of time to put the mark of her breathing, her thoughts, on this room as she reads. The shaping of one's own space, however temporary, can ease the dislocation of travel, and who doesn't need a private anchor in the unknown?

I return to the balcony to see if those students are still there, and just then a strange booming echoes through the air, like the off-rhythm rattling of a distant drum corps. The students below stare off at something down a street that I can't see: maybe there's another, larger group of student musicians that they're about to join.

I turn back to the room, about to say, "We're gonna miss the show if we don't hurry," but I need to be patient, allow Hannah and Alma a little more time. So I give our hotel suite a closer inspection and check out the bathroom, push and pull its smoked-glass sliding door along the runners, press the toilet's flusher, turn the spigots on the sink, all of this the mere busy work of my nervous energy. Then I pull back the window curtains and catch my breath: in the middle of the impressive view of the hill's steep angle up to the university grounds, a huge shifting cloud is rising from the skyline, just a couple of blocks away. What in the world is *that*, I wonder, some celebratory bonfire, perhaps, that other students have started, the ones with all the drums?

I can't restrain myself any longer. "Hey, some kind of party is going on outside. We'll miss it if we don't get moving!"

Point made. We hustle down the hotel stairs, through the lobby and out the door. One short block away, a large crowd gathers in a *praça*, and when police cars and fire trucks approach in a duet of sirens we realize that something Really Really Big must be up. Then, over the heads of the jostling crowd we catch a glimpse of a huge pile of debris. It fills the side street that opens to this *praça*: wooden beams lean at odd angles, and large blocks of stone and broken concrete lie on a rough mound of unnamable dusty gunk.

Alma, ever the anthropologist, lives on the hair-trigger chance of interviewing someone, anyone, so she turns to a woman standing beside us and asks what's happened.

A five-story building collapsed just a few minutes ago is what happened.

That theory about a drum corps and a celebratory bonfire immediately rearranges itself in my mind into the roar and billowing dust of a building transforming into rubble. The woman continues, telling us that the past month of rains weakened the old building and it was emptied a week ago. Though yesterday inspectors gave it a clean bill of health and tenants were already making plans to return. Ah, who took what bribe?—and heads should roll, or at least one, some people in the crowd about us mutter, though from the resignation in their voices I'm guessing that probably no head will ever do any such thing.

Unless, of course, some poor soul lies beneath that wreckage. Already the police, with dogs tugging on leashes, are searching the broken remains.

By now television crews compete with backhoes and cranes, and the police start easing us all away from the scene. Alma, Hannah, and I walk off, more than a little shaken, because if we'd arrived in town only a few minutes earlier we could have been wandering the streets—specifically, *that* street—just as the building tumbled down. Not exactly a close call, but close enough for us to imagine another way our day could have ended. And what other buildings, by the way, might have been undermined by the rain?

We find ourselves entering a long main thoroughfare of shops, lit down the line by Christmas decorations. This, plus the shock of a possible alternate fate, seems to spark Alma and Hannah into holiday-shopping overdrive. I'm not invited (wink, wink), so we agree to meet in an hour or thereabouts, and head our separate ways.

I'm not yet in shopping mode, so I stop at a *pastelaria* and order a cup of tea, with a side of hot milk. Something in my unsettled mood calls up the beginning of a poem by Fiama Hasse Pais Brandão: "Poisamos as mãos junto da chávena / sem saber que a porcelana e o osso / são formas próximas da mesma substância" (We put our hands around the cup of tea / without thinking that porcelain and bone / are made of nearly the same substance). There's a morbid thought that deserves a chaser, so I give some serious attention to the glass counter's display of sweets.

An idle glance at the dessert counter in any *pastelaria* in the country can give you the impression that you've entered a chocolate-free zone, a world where cacao and sugar, like matter and antimatter, don't mix. The Portuguese do indeed know that chocolate exists, and they have some distinctive treats employing the stuff, like chocolate salami, which is a block of chocolate shaped like a thick sausage and laced with crushed hazelnuts to mimic the threads of fat. (It's pork-free physically but not spiritually, and Alma can't bear to look at it.) But when you get right down to it, the Portuguese are a Rebel Alliance defying the Chocolate Empire. What they really specialize in, what captures this country's soul, is a range of desserts called *doces conventuais*: sweets that were first brainstormed in convents. In centuries past, nuns used egg whites to stiffen their habits, and, ever frugal (and because nothing ever gets thrown away in Portuguese cooking), they combined the remaining vats of yolks with sugar and butter. Now the country lives for a dizzying array of distinctive sweets: creamy *pasteis de nata*, the tempting gooey layers of a slice of *toucinho do céu* ("bacon from heaven"—don't ask), tangy *queijadas* and chewy, cinnamon-inflected *broas de mel*, the spongy goodness of a *bolo de arroz*, silky *pudims*, and more, all of them deliciously eggy to the core. They're so scrumptious that sometimes I think God created chickens just so the Portuguese could make desserts.

I keep staring at the glass counter. I don't know where to begin.

✳

The rain has barely paused these past three days, though this Coimbra rain is a parenthetical rain in our lives and therefore easier to walk through. Especially since—right now, at least—we're in Drizzle. We have a few hours to kill before catching the return train to Lisbon, so we're about to squeeze in one more sight: Portugal dos Pequenitos, a nearby children's park, though I'm worried that Hannah might be a little too old to enjoy it.

Our umbrellas perched overhead, we walk past the praça where the backhoe cleanup continues, where crowds still gather, pressing against the police tape. It seems as if everyone living in Coimbra has arrived this weekend to take in the remains of the collapse, and the nearby shopkeepers are delighted with this steady stream of potential customers. What started as a disaster has turned into a happy ending: a building falls in a downtown area and no one is killed, not even a single injury. Rebuilding will commence shortly. Holiday shopping must continue.

It's a clean enough story, scrubbed of major tragedy, and because I'm a writer who breathes in metaphors and symbolism as if they were air, I can't help wanting to shape a comforting parallel, that the disaster of Hannah's school has done her no serious injury, that the debris of her past two months will soon be cleared away and all will be well.

We turn at the traffic light and cross the street onto the bridge over the Mondego River. Below us, the river's dark, cold currents are speckled by our old friend Drizzle. Behind us, on the top of the hill, is the university whose grounds we explored yesterday: the magnificent, overstuffed-with-baroque-goodness library, and the stark accommodations of the bordering student jail that is no longer used but was popular in previous centuries. Drink too much one evening, start an uproar in class, plagiarize a paper, or get caught cheating on a test? Into the school slammer you go. The three of us lingered there a while, joshing about which one of those austere, tiny spaces would be most suitable for the bully Hannah has escaped.

Now across the river, we're finally approaching "Little Ones' Portugal," where kids can run wild among kid-sized replicas of all the country's major historical buildings, representing eight hundred years of Portuguese history. It sounds like a parent's Holy Grail: educational *and* fun.

We'll see.

There's already a line in front of the ticket booth, and after we pay up and push past the turnstile, we first explore a series of disappointingly full-sized buildings devoted to Portugal's various former colonies. This arrangement clearly goes back to the park's first days in the 1940s, during the Salazar dictatorship, when the regime was hell bent on holding on to the empire of its overseas possessions. The displays are stuffed with tacky gewgaws like elephant-trunk umbrella stands, spears, and stuffed animal heads, just for starters. The ghosts of still-vivid colonial wars hover here for too many Portuguese families, who hurry past. So we follow.

Soon we're strolling among pint-sized, walk-through reproductions of the Mosteiro dos Jerónimos, the Torre de Belém, the Sé de Évora, even the university grounds we visited yesterday. Parents may think the place is educational, but kids easily slough off this minor annoyance, because in this magical playground they've had the growth spurt of their dreams. Standing next to these buildings, they're bigger than any adult they've ever met. They bend down to fit through an entrance into cramped interiors, and their faces entirely fill the windows as they peer out. They might as well be giants, yet still they remain kids, as seriously bent on fun as any child should be.

Certainly Hannah has cheered up enormously, even though Drizzle threatens to transmute into Steady Rain. She's by far the oldest child here, and normally this would bother her to the point of bugginess, but right now she can't seem to get enough of striding from cathedral to castle to convent to medieval tower. In a couple of hours our train returns to Lisbon, and tomorrow she'll take her first steps in a new school, but all that seems forgotten now. "Take a picture!" Hannah begs again and again, and whether she would put this in words or not, I'm sure that she feels as if the enormous challenge of this year in Portugal has somehow been taken down a peg or two, made manageable.

Alma holds the umbrella while I continue snapping photos, and some part of me cuts through my symbolic spin and whispers, "Careful, this is not the world, only the way you need to see the world." Immediately another inner voice, the part of me that wants to be as agreeable as possible, adds, "Yes, yes, that's true."

On the other hand, I think, as Hannah runs off to another corner, doesn't the world offer us the raw material for our wishes? How else can we hope, and plan, and shape a near or distant future? Who we are, it seems, is made of nearly the same substance as our illusions.

"Mom, Dad, take another!" Hannah calls out again, and there's our daughter, so grown up that she's taller than the second-story balcony of a country manor; there she is again, barely able to fit in a palace doorway; there she is again, her face shining with an almost defiant joy and framed in the highest window of a water mill.

GO, WHATCHAMACALLITS!

We're on our second circling around the huge Benfica soccer stadium, and my son sits beside me in the backseat of the cab and sighs. It appears I've found the only cabbie in Lisbon who doesn't know where the ticket office is located. At least he says he doesn't—I'm beginning to suspect that he's a supporter of a rival team.

Newly arrived from the airport, Nathaniel would like to begin his winter break by shedding the exhaustion of his transatlantic flight, but I'm balancing the interests of another child right now. One of Hannah's best friends from school back home, Colin, has just arrived with his mother, Claire, on another flight today—they're both big soccer fans, so tonight's game could be one small way to thank them for their visit. Unfortunately, after a couple of days' frustration-nearly-to-tears, courtesy of the team's ticket-sales website, this pilgrimage to the stadium is my last resort.

Benfica's big bowl of a stadium should be like nothing Claire and Colin have ever seen for any soccer game back in the States. The team is ranked smack dab in the middle of Portugal's Primeira Liga elite: along with Sporting and Porto, it's one of *Os Três*—The Three. A sizable slice of players from *Os Três* helped form the roster of the national team for last summer's World Cup competition, which earned a fourth place in the final rankings. No doubt about it, the Portuguese play high-level soccer. Even so, it seems a *little* excessive that, after games involving one or more of *Os Três*, TV commentators will commentate long into the night, and continue the next day, with replays of penalties, goals and near goals, the injustice of injuries suspiciously inflicted, and the eternal perfidy of referees; meanwhile, the three (three!) daily newspapers devoted to local soccer—*A Bola*, *Record*, and *O Jogo*—can go on and on about a single *Os Três* game for eight to ten pages.

The cab driver grumbles, as if it were my fault he can't do his job and locate the ticket office. I'm losing patience to the point where I begin to construct in my mind a cutting remark in Portuguese, when Nathaniel asks, "What's so great about tonight's game anyway?"

"Well, Benfica is one of the best teams in the league, and they're playing the, the . . . um, the Whatchamacallits."

My son throws me the pitying look that he usually throws when I can't remember the name of something and go to the bench for an improvised replacement: whatchamacallit, whoozit, jibbermajabber, whoozamasnooze, thingamabob. Over the years, I've told Nathaniel that I sometimes forget words because of all the drugs I took in college; now in college himself, he's declared this one of the main reasons he won't touch the stuff. (Parents, take note.)

But in this case I have a decent excuse for my memory lapse. The games of the thirteen non-*Os Três* teams in the league get scant post-play mention on the TV news and mere thumbnail write-ups in the papers, if they're lucky. Even after a few months of following Portuguese soccer, I barely know the names of these other teams, much less their players, with the exception of the Belenenses, whose stadium sits a walking distance away from our apartment. I've trooped down to a couple games there and, at least so far this season, they've been ragged affairs, witnessed by a smattering of fans. Months ago, our Portuguese language tutor first tested our conversational skills by asking us to chat about some proverbs, and one of them was *Quer a faca caia no melão, ou o melão na faca, o melão vai sofrer*—"Whether the knife falls on the melon or the melon on the knife, the melon is going to suffer." I'd say that *Os Três* are the Portuguese league's three knives—shiny and sharp with large stadiums, gobs of fans, and tons of money to buy the best players—while the rest of the teams, with so much stacked against them, are often defenseless melons.

I look out the window. Enough is enough: we're about to begin our third circling of the stadium. On a hunch I say, "A esquerda, faz favor"—Turn left, please—and within moments we're parked near the entrance to the ticket office, which stands by itself in a plaza before the looming stadium. I give Nathaniel my own look, a smug smile (I can't help myself) meant to convey equally smug fatherly advice (I really can't help myself): See, there's no need to give up so easily.

I ask Nathaniel to stay put, since I don't quite trust the cabbie to wait. At the ticket window, with my limited Portuguese I pretend my way through whatever swift chatter the woman offers, whatever seat chart she shows me. "Sim, sim"—Yes, yes—I repeat, nodding and smiling until finally I have my six tickets. Not so fast, though—she shakes her head at my credit card, then at my debit card. Cash only.

Is there an ATM nearby? I ask. Yes, she says, pointing to a stadium side entrance. There's one over there, but it doesn't work. Try Colombo, she suggests, which is the enormous shopping center parked across a skein of busy streets from the stadium.

I hustle off in Colombo's direction, where of course there will be scads of machines willing to cough up money for my cause. On the way, I explain my mission to the skeptical cabbie, assure him that I'll be right back. Nathaniel, slumped in the backseat, clearly wishes I'd give up, but I have a long history of rarely doing so, once I've got a bug in my head.

At the street corner, though, I pause when I see it's going to be a haul navigating across some hefty traffic. This whole damn mess *is* taking too long, and Nathaniel needs a nap in our apartment before we head off for the game tonight, so I ask a fellow nearby who's running a stall of everything Benfica—scarves, T-shirts, you name it—if he knows of any ATM that's closer. Sure, in the stadium, he replies. When I mention that the ticket lady told me it's broken, he shakes his head and rolls his eyes, too disgusted to deign further comment at her utter ignorance.

I run past the cab driver again, who now looks beyond stir-crazy, so I shout behind me another explanation and head for the stadium ATM.

Which it turns out really doesn't work. OK, the gods are trying to tell me something, it's time to listen. Releasing any hopes for a soccer game into the chill December air, I slink back to the cab, annoyed at myself for prolonging this stupid runaround.

The driver seems to be stewing behind the wheel at a lower boiling point, and as I slip into the back seat, Nathaniel says, "Dad, he almost left, so I said, 'Faz favor, senhor, meu pai tem instabilidade.'"

(Please, sir, my father is unstable.) Nathaniel grins: "*That* seemed to work." Proud that my son managed to pull this sentence out of his thimble of Portuguese, I laugh, ignoring the consensus that seems to have been established in my absence about my fragile state of mind. Nathaniel must have realized that if he's going to tell his friends back at college about his dad's latest nutty escapade, he'll have to go with the flow and let that escapade happen. We're a team. Inspired by my son's deft maneuver, I lean forward and say, sotto voce (because isn't sotto voce the way you're supposed to speak when bribing someone?): "There's money in this for you, *senhor.*"

Though I've left the promised amount tantalizingly indefinite, he's now all smiles. We cruise the nearby streets until we find an ATM, then drive back to the stadium, and I finally buy the damn tickets.

✻

Later that evening we're part of the crowd flowing into the stadium, at least until I hear the call I can't resist: "Quentes e boooooooas!"— hot and goooooood!—and turn to see trails of smoke rise from a metal cart where *castanhas*—chestnuts—are roasted on the spot. Little stands like this have sprouted up all over Lisbon since the first deep cold of the holidays—Christmas is almost unthinkable without them—and they're almost always attended by a grizzled old guy who, like some living Ghost of Portuguese Past, looks as if he was raised in a tiny village in the mountains. Roasted chestnuts are such a Portuguese *obsessão* that a special celebration is devoted to the first chestnut harvest of the season, and I am so with the program I buy a dozen *castanhas*, wrapped in a cone made from a page of an old telephone book.

Then we slip back into the crowd, pass through the gate, and stop at a concession stand so everyone else can stock up on popcorn, candy, cheese sandwiches, Coke. Eventually we find our seats. The stadium is nearly filled, and I can't believe it, we have some of the best seats—near the field and right by one of the goals. All that trouble was worth it, I think, especially when I look at Hannah and Colin sitting together, chattering away as if no one else existed.

I pick out the first *castanha* from the paper cone and think of a recent newspaper article reporting that these beauties are packed with vitamins B and C and potassium, and have more protein than a potato. Ah, the perfect fast food: healthy, and more fun to eat than any burger or fry. I look at the brown shell that was slit open by a razor before roasting; now it's scuffed with gray ash and the slit has widened, revealing a bit of the cream-colored nut inside, tinged here and there from the flames. I pull at the brittle, warm shell until it crackles and breaks into pieces, and then I have in my hand the nut, shaped like two hemispheres of a little brain. It only takes one bite for me to relish the soft yet resistant texture, and I wonder if this *castanha* is so delicious because I'm eating its slow, patient vegetable dreams.

I pass one to Alma, who loves them too, and another down to Claire, who seems ready to try anything new. The kids shake their heads no, Nathaniel too, and that's OK because I really don't want to share. Each *castanha* brings me back to the sight, feel, and taste of an early memory, when my parents took three-year-old me to the snow-lined sidewalks of New York's Fifth Avenue, to ooh and aah at the department stores' elaborate Christmas window displays. What I remember most, though, is walking hand in hand with my parents past a dizzying wealth of Santas ringing bells on nearly every street corner, then our stop at a roasted-chestnut stand, the feel of the chestnut in my hand, so warm in the cold air, my father crouching down to show me how to pry it open, my mother murmuring praise when I succeed, my first nibble of the treat's delicate taste. It's all so vivid I'm not sure if I'm remembering or imagining.

Our Portuguese friends are surprised and pleased by my chestnut nostalgia—or should I say *saudade*? I remember that evening so longingly because it's one of my few memories of my parents before their marriage began to run on the fuel of bitterness, a fuel that got very, very good mileage. *Saudade*, however, is a complicated emotion, and I believe its mournful notes can be fiercely hopeful too. There's no possible return to that time of my childhood, but I've certainly tried to reclaim its distant happiness in my own family. Alma, sitting beside me, still endures my various quirks and failings, and our children don't (yet) recoil at the sight of me, and what are the improbably long odds of that? Life's not so bad. We have seats with a great view. Good friends are visiting. There are nine *castanhas* left in my paper cone.

The game begins with chanting and drum beating from the stands, and both teams look quite snazzy running back and forth across the pitch. On one side of us, fans of the visiting team wave large flags while warbling the martial cadences of a song I imagine must go something like "Oh great Whatchamacallits, defeat our enemies with a well-placed kick!" I can't help admiring the hopeless nerve of this tiny band of maybe fifty people singing against the entire opposing stadium. On our other side, the Benfica fans start up with their team's song, "Orgulhoso esta bem"—"Pride Is Good," which would be a more impressive tune if it didn't resemble a jazzed-up version of "My Darling Clementine."

At this point I realize that what the ticket clerk sold me are potentially some of the *worst* seats in the stadium. No wonder they were still available at the last minute: we're right smack against a fence I hadn't noticed before, a barrier that separates the thin sliver of seats assigned to the supporters of the Jibbermajabbers from the hordes of Benfica fans. Still, the Portuguese are by and large a peaceful lot, not prone to the sort of violent displays that English or Italian soccer fans are capable of, so most of me isn't worried. The part that's ruled by caution, however, is ready to be surprised.

The hopeful defiance of the Somethingorothers' fans doesn't last long—within fifteen minutes a cluster of players on the pitch before us compete for the ball passing back and forth, until one nimble kick by Benfica's Nuno Gomes sails it straight to the net. Goal! This certainly shuts down the singing and flag waving of that small wedge of fans, and I feel for them. All their out-of-tune bluster couldn't put enough wind behind their goalie's back.

Eventually, the Thingamajigs make a couple of decent attempts at a goal, but by the second half, as one more and then a third goal are scored by Benfica, any distant dream of victory grows ever more distant. I know where my sympathies lie, having always been a supporter of the plucky underdog, all the various Whatchamacallits of the world: the come-from-behind candidate, the terrific book released by a small publisher, the elaborately constructed sand castle facing the incoming tide. Maybe that's one of the reasons I love Portugal, with much of its contemporary literature untranslated (at least into English), its distinctive wines and cheeses unsung, and its keening music—to my mind—insufficiently savored by the wider world.

Though a good twenty minutes remains on the clock, the game

is basically over, and this is probably why, with time and no hope on their hands, the Whoozits fans let their bitterness bubble over. Apparently, some cutting remark nearby has them up and outraged. Insults are exchanged, a few fists are shaken, and it feels as if this spirited mutual contempt is approaching the point where someone, anyone, could turn the Stupid Key, which would unleash all sorts of variations on Stupid, some of them *really* Stupid. I'm not enamored with the prospect of our being caught in the middle of swinging fists or worse, but how to avoid a sudden stampede? Alma and Claire lean closer to Hannah and Colin, and Nathaniel offers me another of his many practiced looks, this one the raised eyebrow of his "Here's another fine mess you've gotten me into" reproach.

Helmeted and heavily padded police appear and line up along the fence, ready to start whacking heads if anyone tries to jump the border. We're nowhere near a riot, though, because both sides seem relieved that this stolid presence of the police encourages an official Calming Down: after all, the Whoozamasnooze fans have had a good howl at the injustice of the world, while the Benfica supporters have thumped their victorious (and rather ungracious) chests.

When the final whistle blows, we begin to make our way out of the stadium, our little group of family and friends still intact and feeling the thrill of danger averted. That's when I notice that the wedge of seats reserved for visiting-team supporters is fenced in up to the walkway and includes a cordoned-off concession stand just for them. They even have their own exit ramp, where off they'll go to their chartered bus, probably under security-guard protection. Sure, it's all for their safety, but it also has the stink of quarantine, as if Benfica fans can't handle a little face-to-face contradiction. Why such sensitivity?

As we follow the streaming crowd out the gate, I wonder if maybe such thin skins come from the Portuguese's long-harbored suspicions that they're a forgotten country, their once globe-spanning empire forgotten as well. You could say they're the Thingamabobs of Europe, who for over two centuries have been overshadowed, invaded, or humiliated by an *Os Três* of France, England, and Germany (I will very tactfully leave Spain out of this discussion). Today the Portuguese strive to hold their own against the cultures and burly economies of these countries, even though the demographics of their smaller nation put them at a disadvantage. Maybe *Os Três* carving up the melons of the soccer league represents for some a spirited fantasy of the Ghost of Portuguese Future.

There's one last *castanha* left in my paper cone. No longer warm when I crack it open, it's still tasty enough, but there's something about my reasoning I don't care for. After all, the various *Os Três* of the world *are* occasionally outclassed and thrashed by the Thingamabobs, and though Portugal may be small in population and square kilometers, it has large reserves of spirit. Me, I've always been about the long odds, and if I were Portuguese, I'd think it my patriotic duty to root for the Whoozits. I glance back and forth, almost nervous to think such a thought, surrounded as I am by Benfica fans besotted with their team's easy victory. No mind readers here, though, so I help maneuver my family and friends across a street thick with traffic, on our way to the metro station, while a Whatchamacallits flag waves in my mind.

Through your heart passed a boat
That without you still follows its course

SOPHIA DE MELLO BREYNER

CHAMA-ME ISMAIL

My daughter takes more than a few hesitant steps with her eyes closed, one hand lightly in the crook of Alma's arm, trying to imagine what it must be like to be blind. She's been doing this ever since moving to her new Portuguese school, which blends blind or visually impaired students with the normally sighted in the classroom; there's a spirit of empathy about the place that's remarkable. Hannah steps slowly, her feet trying out the feel of the sidewalk's landscape of cobblestones.

I'm doing my own navigating, getting us through a crowd of anti-abortion supporters handing out little *Não, Obrigado*—No, Thank You—cards to passersby. Next week Portugal votes on a referendum on whether to legalize abortion, and everyone we know is obsessed with the possible results. There are endless, escalating debates on TV, and the whole country seems cranky. Alma and I, however, can barely suppress our joy at finally escaping the apartment: this is our first outing since we slogged through January with the flu, chilled to the bone. (Like most apartments in Lisbon, ours isn't heated, the price one pays for a tiny carbon footprint.)

We make our way past the statue of Fernando Pessoa and then turn left, to a nearby theater, for the Saturday matinee of a Portuguese production of *Moby-Dick*. I'm still surprised nobody here thought to try an adaptation before, since it's a no-brainer for the Portuguese: their country shares borders with only two neighbors, Spain and the sea, and Spain will always be the least favored. While the sea . . . ah, the sea has for more than six hundred years offered the Portuguese promises of adventure, mystery, and danger, escape from poverty, escape to a new life.

Unfortunately, I'm worried that this play could induce an allergic reaction in an eleven-year-old girl: a whale, a crazy old coot of a captain, and a cast of sailors that collectively probably add up to less than one spoonful of Johnny Depp. Even worse, there's a *very* low prospect of singing or dancing. Hannah's coming along as a good sport anyway, since she's as happy as she's ever been, back to singing in our apartment at any odd moment, having just received from her new circle of friends at school her first invitation to a birthday party—the mother lode of social acceptance.

We present our tickets and make our way to our seats, where the theater's painted ceiling above us is busy with the fluff of eighteenth-century aesthetics—chubby winged cherubs floating between clouds while lush pink nudes loll on beds of flowers. This theater must go back to the times when the Portuguese mercantile empire still ranged from Brazil to Africa, from India to China, an empire fashioned before the invention of instruments that could accurately measure longitude, at a time when conditions on ships were so harsh that often three-quarters of the crew and passengers would die before the final port of call was reached. But something in those days drove the Portuguese *vontade*—will—and imagination to discover what no Europeans had ever discovered before.

The Portuguese also, to their great shame, instituted the modern European slave trade in Africa. Maybe it was karma that caused the wealth accumulated through their empire to be lost over a few centuries by mismanagement and cruelty. Like the rococo excess on the ceiling above us, it's an empire that hovers over the Portuguese today, a ghostly Once Was, a What Might Have Been that could be described as the country's own white whale.

We settle in our seats and page through the playbill, which certainly looks promising, as it includes ten pages of nautical terms, information on the types and ways of whales, and descriptions of the biblical symbolism behind the names of the characters. Somebody's done real homework. Given my slow-lane pace of reading Portuguese, I barely get more than a glance at all this before the curtain rises and the comedic first scene, of Ishmael meeting Queequeg in the boarding house, begins.

I quickly sense something is wrong. First, they've cut the opening line, "Call me Ishmael"—I *so* wanted to hear an actor say, "Chama-me Ishmael." Another bad sign: the actor portraying Queequeg, who wears a tan-colored bodysuit decorated with Polynesian tattoos, seems to think Frankenstein-style grunts are the way to go.

Soon the action moves to the *Pequod*, and it's a little strange watching Portuguese actors portray American sailors, especially since so many of the ship's crew in the background of the novel were Portuguese. At the height of the whale trade, New England ships often sailed out of New Bedford, Massachusetts, with a skeleton crew and picked up the rest at the Portuguese islands of the Azores or Cape Verde, both rich sources of cheap, skilled sailors. The Portuguese were actually the hidden muscle behind the great energy quest of the nineteenth century, so couldn't the playwright have put at least one João or Zé on board?

The stage scenery resembles a Zen version of the high seas, with a three-story tower curved like a prow (or is it the stern?—it's hard to tell) that hints at the rest of the *Pequod*; a full-size mast with a crow's-nest stands isolated in a corner, complete with rope ladder; and there's the bare frame of a rowboat, with wheels, which the actors push along with their feet while exercising invisible oars. Even a three-hour play can't serve up more than a sliver of a six-hundred-page novel, so absence needs to be the aesthetic of the day. I sigh and rustle in my seat, thinking that the best we can hope for is a bonsai version of a redwood tree.

Even so, the minimalism of the sets seems at odds with the declamatory acting style, which rubs out the individual character quirks of Stubb, Starbuck, and Flask. Ishmael disappears as an important character in much the same way he does in the novel, once the voyage of the *Pequod* works up some steam. On stage he's just another sailor with not much to do, but in the novel Ishmael's physical presence transforms into the narrative voice. Here that job has been given to a female character invented for this production: she's a kind of Greek oracle dressed as a Quaker, speaking to the audience directly, intoning some of Melville's more poetic prose about fate and the sea. An interesting invention, this embodiment of all the women left on shore, but the role also feels like a misstep that undermines the necessarily claustrophobic world of the *Pequod*.

Still, the play belongs to Ahab, a captain who is robbed of some essential part of his soul as well as his leg, and whose eloquent obsession with the white whale enlists the crew into what is essentially a suicide pact. No doubt about it, Ahab is a hard role to play, but the actor here interprets him as an unmodulated exclamation mark, an Old Salt leaking out of his shaker.

I know the type. When I was eighteen, I crewed on an eighty-foot staysail schooner in the New England waters. It was a ship searching not for whales but for tourists who were in the mood for a placid cruise from New York to Nantucket, Martha's Vineyard, Mystic Harbor, or Block Island. My captain was Teddy Charles, a former jazz vibraphonist who had played with greats like Charles Mingus and Miles Davis in the 1950s, and he even won himself a couple of *DownBeat* poll awards. Bitter about the rising popularity of rock-and-roll swamping jazz, Teddy plunked his savings into a boat, left the music behind, and ran roughshod over whatever crew came his way—he was loud but also quietly cunning. Sometimes, if I'm in an expansive mood, I like to think of him as a minor Ahab whose white whale had the face of Keith Richards.

At intermission we're released to the lobby, where flat-screen TVs show whales gliding underwater, surfacing, and then diving back to the depths. It's a shock to see images of real whales after the enclosed world of the stage, where, when the hunt is on, the poor actors in that dopey rowboat have to hurl harpoons at an invisible whale offstage. I have a hunch we're not going to see a dramatization of the novel's beautifully macabre chapters that detail the rendering of a whale from a formidable giant into a row of barrels filled with oil. Beside me, Alma and Hannah mutter justly ungenerous opinions about the play, but I'm keeping my mouth shut.

"What do you think?" Alma asks, and I know if I join the club there's no reason for us to stay; we can simply escape out the lobby to the street. While none of my usual optimism can alter the feeling that this play is as doomed as the *Pequod*, a morbid curiosity about its final throes has taken hold of me.

"I think it's pretty good," I reply, with my best straight face.

Back in our seats, we watch Ahab ignore the warnings of one, two, then three captains of passing ships who have had disastrous encounters with the white whale. Stiff neck! He continues the chase, Pip—poor cabin-boy coward—goes mad, and Starbuck from time to time muses portentously here and there on the ship's prow (or is it the stern?). Hannah suppresses her yawns, Alma seems ready to nod off, but I'm pinned to my seat by the slow sinking of this theatrical ship.

Just in time, down comes the white whale from the rafters, attached along its length to three wires, and it hovers over the *Pequod*. There'll be no head-butting with this prop; it looks to be made of a material too delicate for that kind of job. I suppose it's meant to serve as a malign cloud, the cumulous shape of destiny, but the meticulous realism can't quite do the necessary haunting heavy work.

Ahab calls for the chase from that crow's nest in the corner of the stage. Then the whaleboat is launched and Ahab and his crew row off toward the side stage. Don't they see Moby-Dick floating in the air above that abstract prow of the *Pequod*? Hey, throw the harpoons up there! Instead, they fling their harpoons offstage and then creak their way after them. Once they're out of sight, we hear various noises of disaster.

Water starts to leak down the shining metal curve of the ship's prow, a sign that the *Pequod* must have been rammed by Moby-Dick, though the whale's image still floats, immovable, in the air. The novel's feverish, drawn-out three-day chase and battle has been reduced to five lousy minutes of stage time. Curtain down, and there's polite clapping, though not enough to reach the heights of hypocritical enthusiasm. I'll bet everyone in the theater is more than ready to leave behind that hovering whale—and those hovering cherubs on the ceiling.

There's still light outside when we leave the theater, and still the anti-abortion pamphlet pushers remain in force, repelling or attracting passing *lisboetas*. Maybe it's because I've just left a world where harpoons clatter offstage, but I can feel the simmering white whale behind every encounter. This week, one half of Portugal is on the hunt for the elusive, liberalizing spirit of modern Western Europe, while the other half chases after a strengthening of traditional values.

As Alma, Hannah, and I cross crowded streets in search of a restaurant, Hannah goes back to trying out the mysterious steps of the blind, and I find myself wondering what other white whales might be hidden in the people we pass. Maybe this is why the power of Melville's novel has endured beyond the end of the whale trade: we all have our yachts, dinghies, and inner tubes of obsession, malign or benign—a whale, a lost empire, an abortion referendum, rock music, or, in my case, Lisbon. It's a sprawling, friendly whale I've picked, and my daily search for why I love it is friendly, too.

Not so strangely, we're in the mood for seafood, and we stop before a promising *tasca*. Hannah stands before the posted menu, her eyes closed, while Alma reads aloud the specials of the day: *cherne grelhado* (grilled turbot) or *lulas recheados* (stuffed squid) or *bacalhau com natas* (minced cod in a cream sauce). Not a bad way at all to feed an obsession. No danger, I like to think, of drowning here.

ANOTHER HISTORY LESSON

I stop reading out loud, because I've made The Mistake, again. Though I try to back up, my daughter, sitting beside me on the couch, is already drawling her affectionate mudslide of reproach: "Daaaaaad." Then she explains for the trillionth time that *e*, the Portuguese word for "and," is pronounced like the English letter *e*, while *é*, the Portuguese word for "is" (at least—*sigh*—in second-person, present tense) is pronounced like the English letter *a*. Or they're supposed to—I keep mixing them up.

I take my medicine with the proper humility, since her correction is all part of our Study Session Fair Exchange Program. I read aloud from Hannah's history textbook (sixth-grade Portuguese is about my reading level) and cobble together on-the-spot rough translations into English, in preparation for her upcoming test. Meanwhile, Hannah has the last word on my attempts at pronunciation, since she has down pat the music of Portuguese from the back-and-forth of her classroom and playground. Recently she informed me that sometimes, when I think I'm inquiring about *peixe* (fish) in a restaurant, instead I seem to be referring to *pés* (feet). Though I might also have expressed interest in the tastiness of *pais* (parents), *país* (country), or *paz* (peace).

For her previous history test, we'd drilled and drilled in both languages about the fall of the Portuguese monarchy in 1910 and the following struggles and stumbles of the First Republic until the names, dates, and places became permanent folds in her brain. She aced the test, and now she's determined to go two for two, because Hannah, with her usual enthusiasm, has plunged into the life and challenges of her classes (and once again I think of João and Catarina, friends who helped bring about our daughter's midyear entry into her new school—if they were ever to ask, "Oh, Philip, could you please walk through hellfire and back for us, just this once?" I'd do it twice).

Right now we're slogging through the forty long years of Salazar's fascist regime, and I'm impressed how the textbook lays out the case against the dictator with a firm but quiet honesty. When we come to the page about the government's propaganda in the 1930s, I read out slowly the slogan *Deus, Pátria, Família: A Trilogia da Educação Nacional*, trying to hit all the right points of stress in each word. This tactic also gives me time to work up an English version in my mind, and I come up with "God, Country, and Family: The Three Pillars of National Education."

Hannah nibbles on her favorite snack of frozen raspberries in a bowl, and we examine a poster of the time, displayed in the book, that illustrated these words: a father returns after working all day in the fields (though it appears he first stopped and got his clothes washed and pressed) to his waiting, happy family and a rustic home more squeaky-clean than any rustic home ever was. I'm struck by the similarities with the Photoshopped family values of America's right-wing Christians—all glistening goodness, at least as they prefer to present themselves, but these are the folks who carry around wallet portraits of Jesus as a Dorian Gray monster who's A-OK with their war mongering and gay bashing.

Hannah looks up at me, wondering why I've paused, and so I plunge ahead: "Por não haver partidos politicos, a oposição política era considerada ilegal, sendo assim mais facil"—I stop, place the stress on *fácil* back where it belongs, on the first syllable, and when Hannah nods approvingly, I continue—"mais fácil a prática de abusos por parte do poder."

Sometimes it's a hurdle to squeeze English out of Portuguese, but I give it my best try: "With no political parties allowed, political opposition was considered illegal, which made it easier for the ruling party to abuse power." Again, I can't help but think of home, where essentially single-party rule gave Bush free rein to screw up the world. I could say a few choice words about this, but Hannah is fascinated by a political cartoon in the section on *actuação da censura* (instituting of censorship): a wide-eyed woman labeled "Imprensa" (the Press) is sitting in a chair gagged with her hands and feet tied up.

*X*s are inked across the picture, probably the work of some political functionary of the time, and Hannah and I talk about the irony that this protest against censorship was itself censored.

Again, comparisons spring to mind: a bovine American mainstream media chewing the welcome cud of administration talking points, the censoring of scientists over global warming, and the breathtaking chutzpah of outing a CIA agent in order to enforce *omerta*. I'd say all this to Hannah, but she looks tired from the past hour of studying, so we decide to take a little break of volleyball and basketball in the garden of our apartment complex.

The long, grassy stretch is lined with palm trees, cedars, and a number of lush bushes whose flowers will soon be working overtime. This space's feeling of privacy is illusory, since four floors of windows look out over the garden, and maybe that's why it's almost always deserted. Even though there's a perfectly fine bench in an isolated corner, I seem to be the only one who's ever sat there.

We shoot a few hoops, but volleyball is Hannah's sport, and she wants to practice her serve. She gives me tips on how to improve my own, but this is not so successful—the ball flies from my hands in all directions. At least she's getting good exercise chasing my mistakes. I try my best, but I'm still distracted by the too-close-for-comfort implications of Hannah's history book. Sure, the Democrats have finally taken over Congress, but the Lyin' King seems to believe the election was a mere trifle he can shrug off. Some days I've been glued to the Web, following the sordid progress of one scandal after another, and the open sore of Iraq.

While Hannah runs after my latest bobble, I catch the tang of sautéed chicken; I turn to the open window facing the garden and see Alma moving pots and pans on the stove. This year I've been the family cook, chopping, marinating, and simmering during the off moments of my writing, but today Alma—who's usually the homework maestro, in charge especially of math and science—is taking over in the kitchen. Which reminds me, that history textbook is waiting patiently for us back in the living room. I can't say I'm looking forward to the next section, on Salazar's political police, but, hey, studying is studying.

"Esta polícia tinha por função," I read, once Hannah and I are settled again on the couch, "perseguir, prender, torturar e, por" (and

I pause, in order to nail the tricky shush sounds in the next word) "vezes, matar aqueles que se opunham ao regime." Then I give a go in English: "This police unit had the job to persecute, arrest, torture, and, at times, kill those who opposed the regime." Just ten years ago, I could have smugly tut-tutted my way through a chapter like this, but now it has the stink of my own country's shit: the illegal spying on American citizens, the knifing of habeas corpus, and the "enhanced interrogation techniques"—a creepy euphemism that echoes the apple-polished Gestapo term for torture—at Gitmo and Abu Ghraib. How low we've sunk.

At the sound of some polite throat-clearing, I turn to see Hannah's stare. She's waiting for me to return to port from wherever I've been sailing. Well, here I am, sea legs a little wobbly, and finally it hits me: Why not be as honest as this textbook? An old studying trick is to put gobs of information into proper perspective, and we are, after all, a family that often grinds our teeth in synchronous outrage at the politics of the day. So I clear my own throat and proceed to give my daughter another history lesson.

"What Salazar did was a lot like what Bush is doing now," I say, and run through the details of our country's current walk of shame, talking about the parallels and the differences between the two regimes, and soon I can see in Hannah's eyes that the glue of context is working, that this textbook's story from a distant era is finally clicking into place for her.

It's something of a relief when Hannah and I turn the page and finally arrive at the April 25 revolution of 1974. When the fascist government didn't listen to its generals and refused to end the seemingly endless and deeply unpopular colonial wars in Africa, the military finally stepped in. Normally, you don't want to cheer a coup, but in this case the Portuguese military did the right thing—they set up a constitutional convention that established the Second Republic, restored democracy, and in less than two years granted independence to all of the country's African colonies.

My Portuguese friends can display an automatic tick of shame at the mention of Salazar's dictatorship. But the nearly bloodless 1974 revolution is an entirely different matter, because after a couple centuries of hard knocks and awful luck the Portuguese still found the strength to find the best within themselves and make it stick. More than thirty years later, they're still enjoying a noisy, messy, healthy democracy. It was the country's great achievement of the twentieth century, something the Portuguese are justly proud of. Next month there will be a huge party of a parade down Lisbon's Avenida da Liberdade, celebrating the revolution's anniversary. I intend to be there, waving a carnation and wishing I were waving it for my own country.

I sneak a peek ahead and see that we have six more pages to go. "OK," I say, "I think that's enough for now. We'll do a little more after dinner, all right?"

Hannah nods gratefully, reaches for the remote. A little TV is in order, perhaps *SpongeBob* dubbed in Portuguese.

I decide to see how Alma is doing in the kitchen. Steam rises from a pan of simmering vegetables and chicken, and she seems off in her own world. Recently, her new research, on Cape Verdeans with a Jewish heritage (African Jews, whodathunk it?), has taken off, and she's been interviewing up a storm. I decide to leave her to her thoughts, but some small movement of mine catches her eye and she turns to me with one of her wide-open smiles. "How's the studying going?" she asks.

"Good," I reply, though with a bit of a frown because of the depressing resemblances I've been wading through, and when she gives me an asking look, I offer a smile of my own, a rueful expression that promises a story, but later. "I'll be right back," I murmur.

I sneak outside (only for a few minutes, I tell myself) to the lonely bench at the end of the garden walkway. From there I have a beautiful view over the city, the glint of the Tejo River, the far shore. The lights of the 25 de Abril Bridge—named after the decisive date of the revolution—are already shining in the waning sunset. And here's yet another history lesson, the one I came outside for: it *is* possible for a country to right a backlog of wrongs, to purge itself of an extended sickness. The city stretched below me is the capital of a country that managed this and redeemed and reinvented itself for the better. It can be done, it can be.

Alma calls me—where *have* I disappeared to, anyway? "Sorry, be right there," I call back, trying to sound as repentant as possible. I take one last glance at the city below, release an envious sigh, and return down the garden pathway.

WE CAPTURE THE CASTLE

I try my best to resist a sneaky glance out the side window at these mountains I'm driving through, because Alma's "Eyes on the road" mantra waits at the ready if I stray. She's right, of course—what's the upside to plunging my family into a rocky ravine? Still, as we snake our way up one narrow curve after another to the heights of Torre, the tallest peak of the Serra da Estrela, I manage a glimpse at the austere territory below, of wind-scrubbed slopes and stark plains strewn with boulders.

I shift down to first gear for another winding climb, and the engine's grumping briefly drowns out Nathaniel and Emily's backseat chatter. Our son and his fiancée rattle off an impressive string of acronyms—RPG and FPS, RTS and a mouthful of MMORPG—while discussing some computer game they're designing, but the silence of our daughter, sitting beside them, rings louder. I glance in the rearview mirror: head down, Hannah is deep in the world of her latest book. She's read more than sixty so far this year, which fills me with a mixture of pride and concern. Though she's begun a number of budding friendships in her new school, the Portuguese don't quite get the concept of "play date," so Hannah courts imaginary girls on these pages she reads through, snuggling into the thrill of following invented lives, listening in on fictional thoughts. Yet while a first-person shooter or a massively multiplayer online role-playing game might mean nothing to her, I'd bet good odds she'd gladly put her book away if Nathaniel and Emily invited her into their little tête-à-tête.

"Eyes on the—" Alma begins, and I devote my entire gaze back to the road.

My ears, however, are elsewhere. I'm guessing that Nathaniel's steady stream of words back there serves as a protective verbal embrace of Emily. She has bravely accompanied him on his spring-break visit to Lisbon—two weeks of vacation, sure, but also the challenge of trying on a possible fit with our family. I suspect that her calm face, framed by reddish auburn hair, masks an utterly sane wariness. She's certainly heard about our worst behavior, but so far she's only seen our best.

So far. And here we are in our first afternoon of a four-day jaunt into the Portuguese countryside.

"Oh my God, look at *that*," Alma cries, poking my arm. Ah, so *now*, apparently, I can take my eyes off the road? Before I can make some lofty comment on the importance of consistency, I take in a sight that demands the application of foot to brake.

We overlook a small valley shaped like a cupped hand. Huge smooth rocks of different colors, like otherworldly fingers, line the valley's palm, and clear streams cut through strange swaths of moss that range from bright green to dull tan. What really invites exploration is an enormous bas-relief scene carved out of one of the more imposing rocks—the Virgin Mary stands between two kneeling shepherds, their heads bowed as her arms and flowing cape protect them.

I park by the side of the road, and we make our careful way down the mossy inclines, then climb up to the edge of this unexpected sculpture. Even at close range, Mary seems less carved than simply *there*, her astonishing calm shaped from breathing stone. I'm a skeptical type, but I can see how someone of the appropriate persuasion could easily kneel before the spirit of this sight. Soon enough, we turn our attention to the surrounding rocky formations and discover that their black, green, or yellow surfaces are actually the thin crusts of different lichen colonies. Then we turn our attention to the clear streams cutting through stretches of soft moss, we taste the water's cold tang, and it's easy to understand why the Serra da Estrela holds an almost mystical resonance for most Portuguese. On and on, up and down, we wander this small valley in an extended moment of wonder, a family adventure that now includes, for the first time, a fifth person, Emily, and I realize that part of this adventure is the simple fresh fact of her addition.

∗

I'm mulling over that lightning strike of family solidarity the next day, because, as we drive above a narrow river valley toward the small town of Manteigas, Nathaniel and Emily are back in their little bubble, examining on Nathaniel's laptop some photos he took when we'd finally made it to the top of Torre Mountain. Beside the inevitable gift shops in the crisp, rarefied air stood the surprise of two geodesic-dome-like radar towers: abandoned NATO early-warning stations. Now Nathaniel plots how to transform those quaint relics of the Cold War into his own digital versions, for that game he and Emily are planning. Once again Hannah sits beside them, book in hand and odd person out. So at my first chance, I pull off to the side of the road for the promise of a beautiful view of the valley and its swift stream that marks the beginning of the Zêzere River.

No one wants to leave the car, but I nag them out, and all complaining stops when we see below us the river's myriad shallow waterfalls and rapids surging their way through a litter of polished white boulders. "Wow," I say (though from now to forever I'll always see this word in my mind's eye with the Portuguese spelling: *ouaou*). Those miniwaterfalls look so inviting, and the slope to the river, thick with tall grass and clumps of brush, is not so steep, so I wander along the road in search of easy access. "Hey, everyone, I think we can get to the water from here," I call out, and my feet feel the best way down, tentative at the edge of little grassy ledges, at rock slabs with no sure footing.

When I reach the rapids and get over my initial amazement at all the little worlds created by water and stone, I realize no one has followed me. From here, I can't make out the roadside from the clusters of brush on the slope; I call out additional encouragement, but the rushing river swallows my voice. Where is everyone? Miffed, I decide to wander, rock by rock, over the gnarled, twisting water to find a quiet pool where I can brood.

A few minutes of that is enough for me, and I clamber back to the top of the slope, where everyone still stands by the road guard, annoyed at Impulsive Dad, who disappeared, they say, without a word, and never answered when they called and called.

"Hey, *I* called *you*," I begin, then decide to drop it—all I really want is to coax Nathaniel, Hannah, and Emily down there, and soon enough they're off while Alma and I stay behind with the car.

Once they're out of sight, Alma turns and gives me an ample serving of hell, with a side of brimstone, for my sudden vanishing—but quietly, because this is as tough as she gets. A Fernando Pessoa moment arrives, and some of my several selves rise and jostle each other: one Philip protests my innocence, another Philip entertains my wife's point of view, while yet another Philip secretly enjoys the ruckus I've caused. But they all collapse where they came from when Alma tells me how much my disappearance unnerved Hannah. I cave and gush an apology.

That settled, we realize we've lost sight of Nathaniel and company. Ancient parental reflexes kicking in, Alma and I make our way halfway down the slope and keep staring at where we think they should be, willing them to appear from behind a thick patch of small trees or a huge boulder, and they do: there's Nathaniel's narrow frame, then the smaller figure of Hannah, followed by Emily. They're searching together the nooks and crannies of the riverbank, and there, along a rough spot above tumbling water, Nathaniel reaches out a hand to help Hannah, and Emily lifts her from behind.

Then they're waving to us, excited by something Emily's carrying, something so symbolically apt it's hard to believe: even from this distance, I can see the glinting quartz surface of a hefty white stone, perfectly shaped like an enormous egg. They pass it back and forth, gauging its weight, and I want to shout out, "Don't drop that metaphor!" Not to worry—they carefully take turns holding it, as if that unlikely stone were about to give unlikely birth.

✳

The following day, everyone is still a little annoyed at my vanishing act down by the river, so I stick close as we wander the winding narrow streets of Belmonte, past older-than-old women draped in black and equally antique men armed with canes and caps. For a small town, there's a lot to explore: a minor castle belonging to the family of Pedro Álvares Cabral, the first European to encounter the coast of Brazil; a spanking-new and active synagogue (a rarity in Portugal);

and an even newer Jewish museum, which is where we're headed. As the story goes, five hundred years ago the Jews of Belmonte, having been forcibly converted to Christianity, secretly kept alive their old traditions and beliefs. Since the Inquisition in Portugal lasted well into the nineteenth century, only recently have the town's Jews felt safe enough to out themselves.

So we wander two floors of religious and historical artifacts going back to the Middle Ages, in a sleek contemporary setting. One wall lists the names and ages of the 180 or so people who were killed, locally, by the Inquisition: the youngest victim was eleven years old, the oldest eighty-seven. A computer screen to the side of this list calls up tidbits of information about each person, giving contour to snuffed-out lives. Here Alma parks herself, scrolling from life to life, and I'm guessing that she wonders whether some of these people might be related to the Cape Verdean Jews she's been interviewing these past few months. When the Expulsion of the Jews was ordered at the end of the fifteenth century, many who fled Portugal headed for the then recently discovered and uninhabited islands of Cape Verde. There, along with newly arrived slaves from Africa, they began to contribute to the islands' creole soul.

When the museum closes, we make our way along the cobbled streets to the synagogue, where, we've been told, a service will soon be held. Alma must have a ton of questions rattling around in her head that she's hoping to ask, and so she hurries, though it takes little more than five minutes to walk across town. I find myself doubting that any secret could be kept for five hundred years in a community this small. What if the Jews here survived with the help of their Christian neighbors, a mutual, perhaps unspoken pact that lasted twenty-five generations? Now that would be a way, way better story.

At the door, we discover that tonight's service is for locals only. "Come back another day?" says an embarrassed, standoffish elder. "We live in Lisbon," Alma tries to explain, yet it's no go. Centuries of keeping a secret, even if the whole town is in on it, won't encourage admitting strangers at a moment's notice. Though Alma understands this, her face is stiff with disappointment, and she turns away, trying not to show it. We're not fooled. Hannah leans in first, and then we all do, offering murmurs of sympathy to soothe Alma, a brief huddle that seems to do the trick.

*

I'm savoring that collective clinch the next day as we approach a small mountain that rises from the middle of a plain of farmland so incongruously that I can imagine that someone planted a magic stone in a loamy field and it grew and grew into the craggy thing that faces us now. Nestled on one side is the town of Monsanto, whose castle is one of a series of fortresses lined along Portugal's border with Spain. But what really catch the eye as we draw closer are the enormous boulders that dot the mountain's steep slopes.

When we drive into Monsanto and park, they tower over us. Think of a really big rock, the biggest you've ever seen. Now imagine it doubled, trebled, quadrupled, until it's bigger than a house— some are even bigger than a small apartment building. Now imagine rows of homes built around these monsters. Back in the day, the Portuguese must have been real tough bastards, because it takes a certain hardy stubbornness to build a town, a castle, in a landscape like this. Really, if I were leading an army with intent to make trouble for any locals in my way, just one glimpse at Monsanto and its castle perched among huge boulders on the side of a mountain would get me reconsidering the whole pillage-and-destroy concept. I certainly wouldn't want to be climbing a steep grade weighed down with chain mail while dodging arrows and other assorted unfriendly objects. I'd turn to the troops and say, "Forget it, boys—let's go back home to Spain and our women, then kick back on sangria and tapas until we can't budge."

We take lunch in a restaurant that—of course—is built around boulders, and once done, we decide to take on the castle above us. Why not? We'll be storming walls guarded by no one but ghosts, no match for us. When Nathaniel and Emily forge ahead, I try to keep up, until Hannah says, "*Dad*, wait for Mom," and she shoots me a glower that doesn't tolerate back talk. She's right, Alma is huffing up the hill below us. Sometimes, when you're keeping up with one part of your family, you're in danger of leaving another behind. So I sit on one of the smaller of the ubiquitous boulders, catch my breath, and the first sentence of Tolstoy's *Anna Karenina* comes to me, unexpected and unwanted: "All happy families are alike; each unhappy family is unhappy in its own way."

I've never liked the smug simplicity of that opening sentence. What family, however happy, *doesn't* have sadness laced through it? And even families steeped in misery can manage to scrape together a few moments of truce, a sliver of comfort. Any family can swing back and forth between emotional antipodes over the long haul or within the space of a single day, and it's all complicated further by the higher math of all those customized Others that stir inside us. I regard my daughter parked beside me: she's filled with scads of characters from the books she's been reading and the stories she's been writing this year; Nathaniel and Emily, closing in on those castle walls, nurture avatars who'll eventually inhabit their computer-game world; Alma, now only steps away, spends days translating the voices of the Cape Verdeans she's interviewed; and as for me, my fictional buds and I go way, way back.

Alma joins us and for a while we admire together the view of the village below, the odd alternation of those gray smooth curves of rock and red roof tiles. But then a boyish voice inside me rings out, "To the castle!" and I'm off again, braving my way past invisible arrows. Far ahead, Nathaniel and Emily have managed to avoid any imaginary boiling oil flung from the walls, and they enter through the empty space of what must once have been a fully functioning portcullis. Soon the rest of us follow.

We capture the castle. The castle is ours, ours. I look back at the few bands of fellow tourists who trudge up the slope behind us, and I decide, as latest lord of these ancient walls, that my first decree will permit them entrance. My reign here, however brief, will be benevolent.

From inside the castle, we climb the ramparts, for a grand view—the entire surrounding countryside reveals itself for more miles than I can guess. And suddenly I realize—*duh*—that castles once served as a medieval early-warning system, much like those abandoned NATO towers on top of Torre.

I stare in all directions, and there's not a single distant cloud of dust raised by any approaching army. Nah—too medieval, such trouble. Standing here with my family, though, I feel my fretful self worrying about any possible threat that might appear on the horizon, any surprise lurking just around the future's corner that might strain what holds us together. Whatever nameless peril comes our way, we'll certainly have to face it with something far more flexible than stone walls.

I sigh. Do I *always* have to steer through life with the soul of a defensive driver?

Finally sated with the stunning views, we descend to the castle keep and take pictures of each other in practically every combination possible, posing by the cistern, by steps cut through stone. We grin, we stand at attention, we embrace. We continue to create our own supple mix of invisible mortar.

SALVAGE

We're surrounded by glass cases filled with sunken treasure, the kind of booty that pirates would love to get their hands or hooks on: Spanish coins minted in Quito, jewelry studded with emeralds and diamonds, pewter plates, gold cuff links, bottles of cognac and port wine, an astrolabe, a gunpowder scoop, a brass candleholder that adjusts to the shifting pitch of a ship. All of it has been scrubbed clean of incrustations, after centuries underwater in the seabeds surrounding this former Portuguese colony we've been exploring for the past week, the African islands of Cape Verde.

I try to imagine I'm walking along the ocean floor in a diving suit among these neatly arranged treasures, but Alma and Hannah, peering into one of this small museum's glass cases, break the illusion because they're not wearing heavy canvas suits topped by portholed helmets; instead, they've dressed lightly for the African heat. So no invisible fish glide by as I approach a display case devoted to an English ship called the *Princess Louisa*, which sank in 1743 while carrying more than eight hundred ivory tusks. According to the plaque on the wall, as the broken ship lurched on a reef, the crew, convinced that most of them would drown, broke into a shipment of brandy and drank it all, "in order to render themselves insensible to the impending tragedy."

When Alma shifts to researcher overdrive and approaches one of the exhibit's curators with her usual dozens of questions, Hannah slips beside me in front of a glass case devoted to the *Hartwell*. On its way from England to China in 1787, this ship endured a mutiny that lasted three days, at which point the exhausted officers hit a reef off the island of Santiago. Down went the ship, with a huge cargo of gold and silver goods. Before us in the case rest a telescope, two gold watches, and—most touching—a little gold box holding tweezers and such, along with tiny vials of perfume that supposedly retain hints of the original scents. This manicure set is centuries old but also a beckoning future for my daughter, who already longs for the day when she can enter the mysterious rituals of makeup.

Hannah rests her head against the glass and stares. This seems like the beginning of a private moment, so I leave her side and turn my attention to the center of the exhibit's floor, where surprisingly small cannons and cannonballs are displayed. Munchkin weaponry. Not that I'd like to linger in their line of fire, because they're still perfectly fine examples of the perversity of human inventiveness. The case shot on display, for instance, is a tidy package of about a dozen lead balls bound in canvas and resin, ready to be fired into some unlucky ship's rigging; link shot, a close cousin, is a set of twinned lead balls connected by a coiled copper wire, perfect for spiraling through a crowd of sailors on a distant deck.

All that shot went unshot, though—poor defense, in the end, against sudden squalls and hidden reefs, the disasters that brought so much treasure to this museum, riches that weren't meant to stop here but to pass by on their way to and from China, India, Brazil: the once wide range of the Portuguese empire. I continue to wander among the displays of so many ships lost: the oldest wreck went down in 1650, and the most recent in 1850, when the USS *Yorktown*—commissioned to intercept and capture any ships trafficking in slaves—struck an uncharted reef. I pause at the thought of the *Yorktown*'s mission and wonder how many ships packed with human cargo might have sunk in these waters. So many souls lost.

When we leave the museum, I make another stab at that diving-suit fantasy, but it dissolves in the heat, in the beauty of this clear sky over Praia—the capital of Cape Verde, on Santiago Island. So far, this past week has been, for Alma and me, a return to an Africa we've long been absent from. On and off for two decades we had lived in small villages in Ivory Coast, until the fever dream of political and ethnic conflict slowly infected that country with civil war. With the villages of the Beng—the people we lived among—in rebel hands, we haven't been able to return in years.

Yet this isn't the lush West African landscape Alma and I had grown accustomed to. The islands of Cape Verde, parked three hundred miles off the coast of Senegal, are scabs of rock in the ocean. Uninhabited when they were first discovered by the Portuguese in the fifteenth century, and now bulked up with a population of over 400,000, they remain crusted stretches of volcanic soil scorched by frequent droughts. Small terraced farms perch on the driest of mountainsides sloping up to craggy peaks that have been sculpted by millions of years of Saharan wind. Every tuft of green seems like the answer to a personal prayer.

We hail a cab and ride over roads of black basalt stone, past old colonial buildings, gleaming bank branches, and the new soccer stadium, on our way to Sucupira market. Hannah wants to search out one of those local tie-dyed, ankle-length dresses she's had her eye on since we arrived last week—the perfect outfit for her twelfth birthday, coming up in a few days. We step out of the cab, jazzed right off the bat by the typical colors, smells, and sounds of a West African market. Women pass by bearing impossible loads on their heads—bags of rice, stacks of bright traditional cloth—while other women sit on stools or wooden boxes before pungent arrays of fresh or smoked fish, lettuce, hot peppers, onions, fresh bread, cabbage. Music from cassette and CD players tempt us into a maze of stalls (we'll worry about finding our way out later), past the friendly chatter of side-by-side competitors selling flip-flops or sunglasses, in search of that magical dress.

Eventually we stop at a tailor's crowded display, and Hannah chooses a dress of purple patterns that seem to vibrate against the cut of the long white cloth. She sports that classic look of shopping contentment, and I take the opportunity to ask her a question I didn't know I was dying to ask: "So, kiddo, what do you think of Africa so far?"

She pauses a moment, then says, "Africa is beautiful . . . and hard." Hannah has long been a tad jealous of her older brother Nathaniel's stories of African-village adventures with Alma and me when he was only six, and she had been looking forward to this trip for a while. But she's never seen poverty like this, the small, squat concrete homes of the poor ringing the hills, the begging children. Yet for all the explicit evidence of the world's unfairness, there's beauty everywhere as well—the buzz of this market, for one, and above all the confident gait of so many people we pass, their features and skin coloring a singular map of cultural and racial crosscurrents, a centuries-in-the-making creole blend of European and African ancestry.

The afternoon is waning, but ever-energetic Alma has one more spot she wants to explore today—she's heard there's a small section of Jewish gravestones in the cemetery that sprawls along the edge of Praia. Even though I'm a little beat and Hannah looks slightly wilted, we both shrug and agree. After another short cab ride, Alma is chatting up the lanky groundskeeper stretched out by the cemetery entrance. Whenever her research antennae are out, Alma is a super charmer, and I sometimes wonder if anthropology is basically gossip with footnotes.

Eventually, the groundskeeper leads us to a desolate corner where six plain stone markers—half of them chiseled in Hebrew characters—lie flat and partially covered in the sandy soil. They date from the nineteenth century, though there are Jewish gravestones centuries older in the cemetery of a town down the coast called Cidade Velha, a resting place for early escapees from the Inquisition. Alma clicks away with her camera, takes notes, and before we leave we pause, trying to imagine the lives buried there. Then we brush away the sand and respectfully place small rocks on the headstones.

In the evening, back in our hotel room after a three-story walk up, Alma is downloading the photos to her computer when she gets a phone call. "Sim?" she answers, curious about who could possibly be calling, and slowly an I-can't-believe-this-is-happening look spreads across her face. Her hand over the mouthpiece, Alma whispers, "It's the Israeli ambassador to Cape Verde!"

The conversation done, she fills us in. The ambassador has just arrived for his first visit, to present his newly minted credentials to the government, and at the reception afterward he heard about Alma's research from someone she'd interviewed a couple days ago. Small island, small world. And not bad timing, either: he wants to meet tomorrow, which will be our last day in Santiago before we fly to São Vicente, another island in the archipelago.

The next day, we're sitting poolside at his four-star hotel, ordering lunch. This is as fancy as it gets in Cape Verde, and Hannah eyes the kids splashing about nearby. I wish we'd thought to bring bathing suits—she could do with a little fun after being dragged here, there, and everywhere—and I flash her an apologetic glance. She nods her disappointment and then turns her attention to the ambassador, who's handsome in what I assume is the stereotypical diplomat's style: sculpted jaw and a dusting of distinguished gray hair at his temples. He's grumping that the Saudis are building water desalinization plants for some of the islands, but me, I'm more skittish about all the gated retirement communities the Brits and Italians are building on various islands. Sure, construction jobs help the economy, but when the work is done those projects will be just the kind of "look, don't touch" displays of wealth that could bring more than a few simmering poor people right up to boil. The ambassador nods, then tries drawing out tips from us, as if we were old hands at navigating African rituals. We are, in a way, but with a shaky knowledge earned mainly through countless mistakes.

Then Alma mentions our visit yesterday to the Praia cemetery, and he leans back in his chair, suddenly quiet—this is news to him. She's brought along her computer and offers to show him the photos, and soon we're zooming in on the gravestones until the Hebrew characters are large enough to read. As the ambassador translates names and dates, we feel the excitement of recovery, and then he pauses. "This is an interesting epitaph," he murmurs. He points out a line beneath Moises Auday's birth and death dates and reads: *Out of his time, out of his place.*

We fall quiet for a moment at this voice dredged from the past, at this eight-word epic of exile.

✳

I'm sitting in the open bed of a truck because there's no room in the seat up front, where Alma and Hannah sit next to the driver. That's OK by me, since he keeps making stops in the winding streets of Mindelo to collect the musicians who'll be performing today at Calhau, a town on the other side of the island where the restaurant Chez Loutcha hosts Sunday buffets serenaded with live music. It might be a tourist trap, but this is the best birthday party Alma and I have been able to conjure up for our daughter, with the promise of another bash with her Portuguese school friends when we return to Lisbon.

The last of the musicians, a guitarist and a violinist, nod to me as they hop aboard. Then the truck's noisy mechanical soul amps up as we leave town, too loudly for us to do much more than smile at each other. Today's buffet performance must be just another gig for these guys, but for me this trip, with the arid wind whipping through my hair, has the feel of a possible adventure. The island of São Vicente is even drier than Santiago, the clear sky smudged by windswept dust off the bare mountains. An occasional tree or bush offers meager evidence that we're still on a planet resembling Earth. If we don't globally warm ourselves to oblivion in the next century, this is what the world might look like to future humans millions of years from now, when the sun's inexorable expansion into a red giant begins to bake the life out of us.

Then, incredibly, we're passing small farms that dot this blasted landscape, most no bigger than a patch of parched ground bordered by stone walls. Cornstalks stake their fragile claims beside windmills built to salvage unlikely drops of water from an elusive water table, and once again I'm reminded that, in such unpromising terrain, Cape Verdeans have managed not only to survive but to fashion a distinctive culture, one jam-packed with artists. Everywhere you wander, there's music music music emanating from hotel courtyards, café verandas, tiny stages set up in the corners of restaurants, and in the middle of plazas where lovers stroll hand in hand. The major towns on this and other islands are dotted with bookstores that feature the work of local writers, and cultural centers host art exhibitions and original dance and theater productions. Just yesterday, I lounged in a café, sipping espresso while pushing my Portuguese reading skills to the limit with a quite good short story about a man's attraction to a cloistered woman he's never seen, a story I'd picked out from an anthology of Cape Verdean fiction titled, aptly enough, *Tchuba na desert*—Rain in the Desert. Then, as I paged through my pocket dictionary, searching for the definition of *abalroado*—collided—a man with a short-cropped white beard stopped at my table, his face a puzzled squint, as if he were trying to recognize me.

Maybe my own blank look made him blurt out, "Chamo-me Carlos Araújo." He waited patiently for my response, and though his name sounded eerily familiar, still I stared until, on a hunch I couldn't quite believe, I looked down at the anthology in my hands and saw that he was the author of the story I'd been reading. It turned out that he was also the owner of the café. Small island, small world indeed! After a few attempts in my fumble-mouthed Portuguese, we switched to English and discussed art and politics for an hour, while I kept shaking my head at yet another example of the kind of crazy coincidence that has blind-sided, haunted, and delighted me all my life.

Finally, we rumble to the outskirts of Calhau, a small town facing a semicircular bay that curves against the ocean's deep blue. We park in the small lot beside the restaurant, and Hannah jumps from the cab of the truck with a child's coiled energy. Then, almost as an afterthought, she stands as straight and grown-up as she can manage, though the look of that snazzy new dress is undercut by sneakers peeking out beneath the hem.

Inside, long tables lining the side of the large room are filled with tourists from various Scandinavian countries, a British family or two, and a handful of American businessmen. In the center of the room wait the buffet fixings, Cape Verde's typical delicious blend of cuisines, where the Portuguese love of soup meets the West African love of stew, and the Portuguese craze for pork and sausage rubs elbows with African manioc and goat. And that's not including the encyclopedic offerings of fish and shellfish. Even the names of the various dishes sound savory: Cachupa, Canja de Galinha, Carne Gizado, Supida de Xerem.

The musicians have set up by now, and they start to play a beautifully fluid and melancholy tune. Cape Verde's music, like its food, is a thrilling mix, and in any song you can hear the pain of Portuguese fado, the breezy joy of Brazil, and the rhythmic ease of Africa. It's a music that makes you want to dance and weep at the same time, music so beautiful it can make your teeth ache.

The people sitting around us, though, want to chow down and listen, not dance. I'd love to grab Alma's hand and lively up the joint, to work off some of this great grub, but this would surely mortify our daughter, and it *is* her birthday. So I content myself with the memory of the night last month in Lisbon when Alma and I took in the music of Boy Gé Mendes at a Cape Verdean nightclub, a venue that was once the comfy home of a seventeenth-century family of the Portuguese nobility. This home, which had likely been built on profits from the labor of slaves in Cape Verde, Brazil, or elsewhere in the Portuguese empire, was now claimed by the descendants of those slaves, and their transforming music ringing off the walls offered an irony so gratifying that Alma and I found it impossible not to step out and pretend that we were even one-tenth as good as the couples who carved out breathtaking territory on the dance floor around us.

The music pauses when the hostess approaches our table and sets down an oversized cupcake topped with a sparkler that sparkles itself down to nothing, leaving one lone candle for Hannah's wish. Then the band starts up with "Parabéns a você," the Portuguese version of "Happy Birthday," and as everyone in the room joins in, her face flushes with embarrassed pleasure at being the restaurant's brief center of attention.

The feast finished, we stroll outside the restaurant for some fresh sea air, and Hannah settles into one of the veranda's hanging chairs, made of hemp and ripe for swinging. Alma and I take turns pushing her, and it's a moment to savor, parents indulging in their child's pleasure. There are precious few remaining, I imagine, since Hannah's new age of twelve tacks just a little too close to the dangerous reefs of Teenage Wasteland. Soon we'll likely have limited chances to salvage a moment like this except in memory, reclaiming our daughter's fading childhood as if it were a cluster of sunken gold coins.

We continue on to the water's edge, examining the ebb and surge of the volcanic beach's various small tidal pools. In the distance, the uninhabited island of Santa Luzia seems to rise out of mist, and behind it loom the cliffs of a larger island, São Nicolau. Following her curiosity, Hannah wanders along the shore, then stops as a windy gust snaps the folds of her long dress. She sweeps tangled hair from her forehead with an assured gesture, and I blink my eyes: she seems years older, the young woman she's about to become. Alma catches her breath beside me and I'm sure she's thinking this, too. Hannah sees our gawking, begins to walk back, and then—a surprise—she *skips*. She skips, and I count each step.

LIGHT FOR LIGHT

"So, Philip, what do you think of these socks?"

I'm sitting at Rui Zink's kitchen table, where piled before me are the latest examples of his generosity—a DVD of an obscure Andrei Tarkovsky film, a Sandman graphic novel—and I try to process the sight of him standing in the apartment doorway, each black pant leg pulled halfway up his calf to reveal a bright white sock.

"They seem to fit," I reply, still not sure what he's getting at with this sartorial display.

My friend's broad face deflates a little, because he's trying out a joke for tonight's show. And what a show it is. Rui is a cool guy (though his last name *does* sound like a Dr. Seuss character), the kind of writer who'll take on anything: stories, novels, essays and political commentary, plays, graphic novels. His latest gig is in that eclectic spirit and beyond, because he's serving as a judge for a reality TV show, *A Bella e o Mestre*, a Portuguese version of an American show called *Beauty and the Geek*. Dumb and lovely gals pair up with smart and geeky guys to compete for a prize of one hundred thousand euros, and, as one local newspaper wryly observed, "Elas são bonitas, eles são inteligentes e o contrario não é verdade"—"The women are beautiful, the men are intelligent, and the opposite isn't true." It's the country's most popular TV show right now, and Rui sees it as a great ironic leap into the belly of pop culture. He'd like everyone to be in on the joke, but I've met too many folks resistant to the show's charms. Just the other day, at the mere mention of the program a mutual friend of Rui's and mine opened her mouth and pointed a finger inside for a spot-on pantomime of retching.

Rui goes back to fussing about this and that, ranging the rooms of his apartment—the necessary jitters before a show—until the phone rings. Rui picks up and tells his driver (now *there's* a sign of TV stardom) that we'll be outside right away. We hustle down the stairs of his apartment building, and I brace myself for a dose of staged American reality with a Portuguese accent.

Though I heavily favor the finger-in-the-throat point of view, I'd follow Rui just about anywhere, he's that kind of friend. He's introduced me to fabulous hole-in-the-wall *tascas*, out-of-the-way bookstores, and a gaggle of composers, filmmakers, magazine editors, comedians, and musicians, and tonight our destination is a TV studio near Mafra—a town famous for the huge, beautiful convent whose construction gobbled up a sizable portion of Portugal's wealth in the eighteenth century—where the latest episode is being filmed.

There's the company car, parked across the street, a blandly normal man and a stunning woman standing beside it. At first I peg this pair as contestants, but Rui introduces them as two of the show's producers. Which is odd, because the first thing the fellow says to me is "It's such a stupid show," followed quickly by his colleague's "Oh yes, such a stupid show." Rui gleefully nods agreement.

Before we can leave, though, some sort of negotiation sets in, cell phones are out and calls are being made. In the current state of my Portuguese I can make out the fuzzy outlines of what's being said while the tricky details lose me, so at moments like this I settle back into silence and wait to see if the conversational knots tighten or unbind. Rui leads me aside to explain that he neglected to mention he'd invited me along. Because the producers weren't expecting me, it seems I'm taking someone else's place in the backseat. I offer to visit the show another day, but Rui shakes his head. "No, trust me, I have to play the prima donna now; it's the only way things get done in their world."

Oh Rui, I think, don't lose yourself in this part, but I keep it to myself and simply nod. Finally we're off, though I'm not sure anything has been settled. As we pass through Lisbon's narrow streets I forget about backstage politics, because the beauty of the city's nooks and crannies always puts me in a meditative mood. I take in swift glimpses of rows of tiny shops, ranging from narrow *pastelarias* to pocket-sized hardware stores to clothes stores barely larger than a closet, each artfully brimming with inventory, because the Portuguese know as well as the Japanese how to sculpt a tight space. Then we're barreling down a broad avenue darkening from the shadows of evenly spaced trees cast by the setting sun, then we pass a park a fountain a café.

The producer stops the car on a side street in front of some sort of warehouse, and the cell phones pop out again for more mysterious negotiations. Rui and I step out to stretch our legs, and he's back to pacing—it's getting dark and still we haven't left Lisbon. We wait until a middle-aged woman sporting reddish-brown hair, accompanied by an off-white plug of a dog, approaches at a confident clip. Rui introduces her as Clara Pinto Correia, one of his fellow judges.

Clara sizes me up with a wry look and then says in English, "Welcome to tonight's descent into hell."

Well, that's certainly stronger than "It's such a stupid show," but before I can reply there's a brief anxious to-do about who fits where in the car. Rui sits up front beside the bland producer, I get to sit in the back between the stunning producer and Clara, while her dog is relegated to the open trunk space behind us. So I finally catch on: the pooch was my rival for the free seat.

Clara doesn't seem to hold it against me. The moment the car starts up, she turns to me and starts up too, words and words and words she can't stop. "Oh, this experience has been so revolting, so horrible, how to endure it? I can't stand it anymore, the depths of the contestants' stupidity keeps me from sleeping at night, what does it say about the state of our educational system?"

By the time we're on the highway Clara's still at it, telling me she's a fiction writer as well, who also teaches biology at the university but how can she teach when she's so preoccupied with this ridiculous show? "So I'm quitting, tonight. Why wait? There are no more surprises to be had, this show is only going to reach lower and lower levels of degradation. Besides, I intend to write a novel about the whole sorry experience, and I've already collected more than enough material."

She's in full venting swing, and I decide the right conversational strategy is to simply nod and line up a polite queue of ums and uh-huhs. Rui shifts uneasily up front. He's not immune to Clara's complaints, but he's had enough, and suddenly he's humming, low at first and then louder, building a buzz of off-key melody in his head that will drown her out. In the boot behind us the dog, perhaps in sympathetic response to her master's low growl of misery, begins a counterpoint of whimpering. The two producers sit pinned to their seats, silent amid this harmony of grumbling, humming, uh-huhs, and doggy whining, but I'm getting used to it, keeping up my part while hoping the turn-off sign to Mafra will show up any minute.

A child's sudden wailing interrupts our *musique concrète* collaboration, and I nearly leap out of my skin. The sound comes from the beautiful producer sitting to my left, but her mouth is closed. Again a little girl's voice cries out, "Mãe! Mãe!"—Mama! Mama! The woman pulls out her cell phone and answers, "Sim, querida?"—Yes, darling?

I'm staring at her, and though my mouth must be open wide, must be, no words will come. When she finally signs off I manage to squeak out, "That's some ring tone."

"Yes, it's my daughter's voice."

"Your daughter's?"

"Her voice, yes. She's only two and a half, and when I work at night she misses me, and I miss her too, you know?"

I nod, remembering how the lonely cries of my son and daughter when young echoed inside me. "Well, that's a ring tone that'll certainly get your attention," I say. "Now that I think of it, it's perfect, really—even if your phone goes off at the worst time, who couldn't forgive a mother the cry of her child?"

I'm babbling. She smiles wanly, then turns to the window.

None of this has put the brakes on the dog's quiet keening, and now Clara starts up again, the entire show has been a humiliating experience, her friends won't speak to her, and I'm back to my uh-huhs and Rui returns to his humming. This finely meshed production is so in gear that when the little girl's recorded voice cries out "Mãe! Mãe!" for a second and then a third time none of us bother to pause, and still we barrel through the dark, Lisbon now far behind us, the town of Mafra who knows where in the distance.

✳

The studio space is shaped like an amphitheater that's split in half, with the women in the audience seated on one side, the men on the other (though for some unknown reason a few guys behind me are cross-dressed as false-bosomed pirates with leopard-skin tricornered hats). Below us in the center of the set, while eight cameras cover every angle, a no-nonsense prompter with a Brazilian accent guides us through the niceties of the synchronized cheers and applause he expects us to master before the show begins. I'm having trouble concentrating, though, because I can't stop staring at two women on the other side of the audience who each wear a stark white mask, unnervingly expressionless. I wonder if they're here to cheer on a relative but don't want to be recognized by friends or coworkers.

The show's hosts appear—a painfully thin woman who must live on dabs of air spread over cloud crackers, and a fellow with a goofy grin who's nearly as skinny—and they unwind some scripted chitchat for us until the four judges arrive. Clara strides onstage along with her dog (on her last show, she'll do whatever she wants), followed by Rui, then the essayist Carlos Quevedo, and finally Marisa Cruz, a slinky blonde model, and I'm reminded why I love Portugal, a country where the presence of three writers defies American reality-show judicial tradition.

Rui tries out his white socks gag, a lack of fashion savvy that draws the audience hoots he'd hoped for, and then the contestants march in, busty young women balanced in low-cut dresses, accompanied by guys who put the *A* in awkward. They're followed by couples wearing jaunty white banners stretched across their chests that announce ELIMINADO. No anonymity for failure on this show.

The contestants get down to business, the geeky men proving themselves beginners at miniature golf and archery, while the women struggle to identify images of famous people projected on a large screen. The imperious stare of Margaret Thatcher draws a blank, and the closest guess one beauty can manage for John Lennon is Elton John. The poor souls can't even recognize images of koalas or flamingos, and the folks I'm sitting among are an unruly bunch, guffawing at such egregious ignorance and offering rude backseat advice. They even comment on Carlos Quevedo's Spanish accent: "Fala portuguese!"—Speak Portuguese!

At the break I'm guided backstage and up a flight of stairs, and everyone on the crew seems to know about me—or at least my country of origin. "*You* invented this!" more than one joke reproachfully.

I flash a smile that aspires to sheepish and ease past. I wouldn't mind making my own crack, because cultural influence works a two-way street. Alma and I recently threw a belated birthday party at our apartment for our daughter with her Portuguese school friends, a couple hours' worth of pizza, rap music dancing, and hula-hoop high jinks. An Americanized do on the surface, but I knew that Hannah—athletic, tall for her age, and standing out among her school friends—wished she could shrink herself down to the impossibly small package of a Portuguese girl (never mind that the whole country qualifies as the shrimps of Europe—only the island of Malta boasts smaller citizens).

Backstage in the judges' roost, glasses of whiskey and cups of espresso pass around, Rui takes charge of the discussion, and I'm a little surprised at how easily it's decided which couple looks headed for the chopping block. Then we all return to the studio set for the second half of the show, and Clara announces her departure, loyal dog by her side for moral support. While I can't quite follow what Clara's saying, surely her brief speech is a tad more tactful than her grumping in the car, because when she's done the audience rises for a rousing ovation.

When the applause dies down, the two hosts lead Clara to the hot seat before the large screen and ask her to identify images of pop culture—apparently not her strong suit, as she's stumped by the hunky male actor from some daily soap and the prepubescent singing star. Clara takes it all in with embarrassed grace before she exits, and then only three judges remain, left behind to judge more of the same.

✳

After the show, a subdued Rui and I munch on snacks in the backstage cafeteria, the contestants and *eliminados* mingling about, and he points out this fellow's or that young woman's back story or personality quirk with his usual writer's eye for detail. I sit back and listen, certain that Rui knows he's in too deep, that the supposed joke of the show is costing him. But he's no quitter—he'll stick it out to the end and see where it takes him. He's a beast for experience, that's for sure, and if any novel ever gets produced from this mess, I think I'd prefer it be written by Rui.

Carlos joins us at the table and nibbles on some chicken. It's late, and he and Rui look tired. They've punched the clock at the American Cultural Factory and done their time, so we head outside, and it's just the three of us that the bland male producer chauffeurs back to Lisbon.

I sit in the front seat, Rui and Carlos stretch out in the back and try to shake off the show by yukking it up and cracking open cans from a six-pack of Sagres beer that Rui commandeered from the cafeteria spread. I take pulls from a can too, but I'm quiet, off in another place and time. Strange, how our past travels travel with us. Years ago when Alma and I lived in our first small African village, the only Westerners for miles and miles, it turned out our neighbors held certain preconceptions about us, drawn from action movies that young men in the village had seen in larger towns when they'd served in the army. Everyone assumed I knew karate, and that Alma and I owned a handgun, secreted somewhere in our mud-brick house. Didn't every American pack heat, as a backup in case the latest karate brawl wasn't going well?

Eventually I convinced the young men, hungry for lessons, that I'd always been karate chop challenged, and we kept repeating to our neighbors that we were firearm *un*friendly, but no matter: at the end of our fifteen-month stay the villagers competed for the privilege of buying our nonexistent gun. Though we had learned to speak well enough to communicate more than a glimpse of our essential selves, had spent hours each day dispensing free medicines, the images from American movies—which only a few people in the village had actually seen—somehow trumped us.

I take another swig of beer as we speed down the highway, depressed at the thought that wherever we Americans venture abroad, whether we like it or not we wear a crackling full-body halo (apparently invisible only to us), an aura shaped of car crashes and gunfights, horror-movie monsters, martial art acrobatics and gangsta posturing, gaunt haunted fashion models, all manner of inventive ka-booms and ka-blams, grainy porno close-ups, and now—thanks to the little emperor from Texas, bent on setting the world on fire— torture cages and carpet bombing. I'm my own blazing Fourth of July, I think.

Rui and Carlos still murmur and chuckle to each other in the backseat, old friends tending to current wounds over the last cans of beer.

Lisbon eventually comes into view, and its faraway lights shimmer in the night through the trees we pass, flickering like muted fireworks. I sit up, charged by this illusion, and then, thinking ruefully of my own pyrotechnical display, I realize I match the city's distant dazzle light for light.

ESTE ESPECTÁCULO CRUÉL

We're lost, driving slowly right and left and every which way through the streets of Santarém at ten o'clock at night. We're tired, too— what with Hannah's full school day and Alma's Cape Verde research lecture at a Lisbon university—so I try my best to tease out the logic of the town's confusing roundabouts, which lie between long streets running the length of lovely parks, still hopeful that the hotel we're searching for does indeed exist. Alma stares once again at the map and, sparked by some unexpected insight into the printed web of streets, suggests a series of turns that ends up getting us where we're going.

We lug our suitcases into the lobby, glad to check off this first leg of a five-day jaunt to the north of Portugal. We chose Santarém for starters because Alma discovered online that a church here boasts the 760th anniversary of some miracle, and the town currently hosts an agricultural fair we might wander through, so we have lots of questions for the grizzled fellow at the reception desk. He isn't much for eye contact, though, and he might even be mute—not the ideal career choice for a man of less than a few words. When he slurs out a few syllables that might be a response to our own simple Portuguese, it's clear that he's not drunk but damaged somehow. Alma notices on the wall behind him a large clock in the shape of Africa, unusual next to otherwise traditional Portuguese decor, and she whispers that he might be a shell-shocked veteran of the colonial wars.

I sneak a sad glance at him, and then pluck a booklet on the town's agricultural fair from a pile on the reception desk. In our room, I page through the schedule—the whole shebang is open until the wee hours. I'm still charged up by a decent day of reworking a novel chapter. When I read that a *largada de touros* will take place at 11:00, a quick flip through my ragged pocket dictionary tells me this means exactly what I suspect: Release of the Bulls.

Now, this is something I've always wanted to see, although from a goodly gore-safe distance. Alma, poor soul, sighs and shakes her head at the mere suggestion, and Hannah's too tired to even consider extending our long day. They decide to stay behind, maybe play a game or two of Boggle before turning in, but I'm not allowed out the door without first swearing absolute scout's honor not to get myself bluntly aerated.

With more than a little hesitation, I ask the fellow at the reception desk for directions. He mumbles a word or two without raising his eyes, then writes down a few cryptic squiggles of what he's not further inclined to say. This is enough, it turns out, to get me there in just a few minutes. I park the car beside the monumental building that houses the fair, its curves and pillars a dour modern version of a Roman temple. Even so late, this palace is packed inside with families pushing strollers, teen boys eyeing teen girls wearing cowboy hats, middle-aged men traveling in groups of three and four without their wives. Rows of stands serve local food and wine, around the bend there's a small petting zoo of sheep and goats, and everywhere traditional crafts are for sale. Ah, shopping—just the fulcrum I need to pry Hannah, and therefore Alma, out of that hotel room. I call to wheedle them into letting me drive back and pick them up (there's still time, I point out), but my attempted charms get nowhere.

I wander alone until I catch a whiff of something that plugs into deep memory. The words *hot dog* and *baseball* rise up inside me, and I'm back to long-ago outings at Shea Stadium, where I watched the Mets—despite all my hopes—lose and lose again. The lip-smacking scent beckons from a booth selling grilled sausage, and after a glance at the chalkboard menu I order a chorizo sandwich. The young woman beside the register squints at the question mark of my accent, which pegs me as a way-way-out-of-towner, a type local agricultural fairs don't normally draw, so I repeat my order, she finally nods, and I plunk down my euros and sit at a picnic-style table to wait.

What finally arrives is not the sandwich I thought I'd ordered (what tripped me up—pronunciation? grammar? both?) but a mound of three types of bite-size sausage pieces, some already help-fully pierced by toothpicks. I take a tentative stab at the greasy mor-sels, trying first a black blood sausage, then a fiercely red and chewy chorizo, then a tan and softer version. They're each delicious, scar-ily so, because if I somehow allow myself to eat everything my heart will surely shift down to a single ventricle. After digging a respect-able dent in the meal, I return to the booth to ask the young woman, "Faz favor, onde fica a largada de touros?"—Excuse me, where's the release of the bulls?

I walk down the sloping field where she pointed and pass a clutch of flimsy-looking food stalls, then take mental notes while strolling past a display of imposing farm machinery—those gleaming tractors and threshers might offer me a nook of safety if I later return this way only steps ahead of a pair of sharp horns. Finally, I come to a large wooden circle of a building. A bullring—I'm at a bullfight? Apparently, "release of the bulls" doesn't mean a barely sane free-for-all. Instead, I walk among farm families as I search for a seat, past sleepy children cradled in their mothers' arms, buddies jostling and joking, shy first dates, and a hawker touting creamy *queijadas*.

In the middle of the ring, there's some sort of theatrical perfor-mance in full swing, and I find a seat and watch two lovers trade ex-aggerated embraces and accusations. Then a pair of lean, mean actors exchange threats and mime a knife fight until three sultry dancers, skirts flaring, slink across the bullring's sandy soil, each twirling a rack of horns. Urging a would-be matador not to take up the cape, one statuesque beauty rails against "este espectáculo cruél!"—this cruel performance!

"Shut your mouth and hit the road!" a fellow beside me shouts out, to nearby chuckles. The folks here behave as if they're at home josh-ing a TV screen, and the acting before us is certainly *telenovela* style: those earnest, longing looks and grand gestures are designed for the farthest seats. In between these hammy scenes, from a small stage fit into the stands, a handful of fado singers take turns belting out songs with a tight band. Whether homebred or a traveling troupe of musicians, they're damn good, pounding out muscular, passionate music that's as punk as fado gets.

When the bull finally enters, through a swinging gate, a couple of matadors ease into the ring and wave capes. Years ago, I took in a night of bullfights at Lisbon's Campo Pequeno, so I know these guys serve as mere warm-up, an attempt to wear down the bull a bit before the main event of eye-popping equestrian feats. Sure enough, a *cavaleiro* soon enters, perched on a fancy white horse, its mane and tail braided, and he takes a few turns to provoke the bull's charge. The horse canters sideways, even backward, guided by the *cavaleiro*, staying mere inches from the horns of the bull (the tips are blunt, but they're not playthings). Then, with a flourish, that *cavaleiro* reaches into a quiver of spears sporting colorful streamers and, horsy hairpin turn after hairpin turn, he pins them into the fleshy hump of the bull's back.

In the face of this bloodletting designed to further fatigue the bull, I'm grateful my cell-phone pleading fell flat. By this point, Hannah would have held palms over eyes and fingers in ears while Alma led her out of the ring, not without a glance of utter disappointment at me first—yet another chapter of Father's Failed Adventures we wish had never happened. I would have followed, chastened, but an unexpected drama holds me here now. That bull down there is one reluctant beast, more confused than angry.

Between provocations, he, a seemingly meditative soul, wanders back to the now closed gate where he had entered. This bull just wants to go home, wherever and whatever he imagines that to be. Yet something also stirs within at the approaching horse's challenge, and he can't help himself, he charges again, however disappointing the result. Clearly, this is his first bullfight. Then I realize he has no idea what's coming next because *every* bullfight is a first, for every bull. There's never a rematch. The entire spectacle is the waving of a wand of human cleverness just beyond each animal's blundering ken.

Finally, the finale—and the closest any bull will ever get to a fair fight. Eight local fellows, amateurs all and ranging from scrawny to pudgy and flashed up in matador style, form a single file facing the worn-out bull, and the fellow in front stamps his feet, inviting the inevitable charge. Then that first guy throws himself on the bull's lowered head, clutching the horns while the rest rush three to each broad side of the bull, the last fellow taking tugs at the tail, and they keep up this crazy crowding until the exhausted creature simply stops, subdued but still standing, one last humiliation.

The local heroes bow and wave and exit. The poor bull stands there in a bright spotlight beside the curve of the ring, tips of festive spears dangling from his bloody back, while farmers sitting around me crow insults. He has no idea why any of this has happened to him, and he waits, uncomprehending, for who knows what might follow, while a fado singer rips through another song. Usually, the bull is led out of the ring to be dispatched in private later, but maybe tonight there will be more to this *espectáculo cruél*; maybe folks will be invited down to the sandy ring for this tired animal to roam about after them. No longer interested, I rise to leave and ease my way sideways through the stands.

*

A turn here, then a turn there through the stark crags and chasms of the glorious Gerês Mountains, but still we can't find the curiosity I'd uncovered in one of our guidebooks: a *fojo do lobo*—a series of stone walls, built in the Middle Ages, that once served as a wolf trap. Alma keeps glancing back at Hannah, who is curled asleep in the backseat. Our daughter's not the napping type, but she deserves whatever rest she wants: though all her classes are in Portuguese, Hannah's grades are among the highest in her school.

We've come so far—and so close, according to the guidebook—that I don't want to give up yet. At the height of one wooded hill, I park the car, then march about in search of a clearing. Peering in all directions, I can make out, to my right, the rooftops of Fafião, which we passed a half hour ago before circling through these mountains. The village's narrow streets, lined with stone buildings that seem as if they've been in place for thousands of years, remind me of the stories of Miguel Torga, a Portuguese writer I've been rereading recently. Torga died before his many nominations for the Nobel literature prize could snag him the big one, and he was robbed. I've always admired the rough-hewn poetry of his prose about peasants who, in remote and unforgiving mountain landscapes, were "born poor, lived poor, and died poor."

I turn from Fafião and squint at the wild terrain below, until I see a dark line or two that seem to fit and yet defy the natural contours of a nearby hill. I mark it in my mind and hurry back to the car, where Hannah still sleeps in the backseat. Peering in the window, I'm not sure how much I should worry about her recent hunger for rest. Off and on since our trip to Cape Verde, she's complained of stomach pains, but a couple of doctor visits haven't turned up a thing. As I ease into the front seat, erasing my concerned face, I whisper to Alma, "Last chance, and then we'll turn back, OK?"

After reaching a dirt road that leads along the bottom of that hill I'd scoped out, I park and half-close the door so I don't disturb Hannah. Off I go, not quite sure how this terrain fits with what I saw back on the ridge, but on a hunch I take a turn up a path on my right, past low scrub brush and sandy soil exposed in the midday sun.

I'm halfway up the hill and there they are: two stone walls, eight feet high or more, parallel and far apart, leading away from me. I approach one wall to examine the fit of stones, each of which balances against the others without mortar. Within any gaps, shards of smaller stones snugly, perfectly fit, and I gasp at the enormous care behind this construction. It reminds me of a passage in one of Torga's stories describing villagers who, "inured to long slow hours, are as patient as watchmakers, and full of ponderous scheming. As in the planted fields, where for long weeks one can stare into the same motionless meditative enigmatic cornstalks, secretly ripening, so in the dullest slowest stodgiest most placid and silent men there lives, at times, a secret determination to create and ripen."

I continue along the wall, see how it eventually turns down a gully and narrows the gap between it and the second wall, the two finally leading to a deep stone pit that poses the final trap. The pit below is overgrown with weeds, and I can understand such neglect—who would easily venture down there among the souls of so many angry wolves?

I wonder how our friend Sónia—a biologist who studies with great compassion the last remaining wolves in Portugal—would react to this place, and again I'm thinking of Torga's stories, where farmers know their sheep individually, "as if they were people," and when a priest's homily berates his backward congregation, claiming that come Judgment Day they'll all be sent to hell and only the sheep will be spared, the villagers weep—not for themselves but at the thought of their flocks left behind with no one to defend them from preying wolves. This *fojo de lobo* goes beyond some elaborate architectural exercise. It's personal.

Then I remember that Alma and Hannah are still back in the car. I flip open my cell phone and call. "You and Hannah just have to see this," I say, though I doubt I'll get much traction. For my wife, a child's sleep is the Fountain of Youth, El Dorado, and the Promised Land all rolled into one, so I'm shocked when she agrees to wake Hannah. I hurry back down the gentle slope of the hill to make sure they take the right path through the sparse trees, and as I lead them back a bell goes off inside me. The first time I saw these walls, I was impressed mainly by their construction, but now, this second time around, I see why someone, long ago, carefully picked this particular terrain to build a *fojo do lobo*. I see the cunning of the walls' placement.

I'm no expert on wolves, as Sónia is, but standing here I can imagine a long-ago drama, imagine that barking dogs and shouting men behind the fleeing wolf are just noise to him because he hasn't begun to break a sweat—he can go on for miles. So he barely notices the stone wall, parallel to his running and far to his right, which disappears over the horizon of this hill he's climbing, and he barely perceives the wall far to his left, which seems to end abruptly at the hilltop's distant curve. Instead, he keeps his eyes on the promising view before him of the forested mountains beyond, where he can escape, and then return another day for another sheep.

So the wolf continues dashing up this hill, unconcerned, until he reaches the crest, where he finally sees what he couldn't see before. That wall on his right takes a sharp turn to the left, cutting him off from the mountains; it's a tall barrier that continues along the downward slope of the hill. But the second wall, on his left, has apparently ended, so he runs in that direction, only to discover again what had been just out of his sight: it, too, has veered sharply to the left, also down the slope. Racing back and forth, he discovers that each high wall resists his leaping, while the howls of the dogs and the shouts of their masters draw closer.

He can only try to escape to where the walls on each side slowly narrow his possible path until they appear to leave an opening he can fit past. Yet when the wolf rushes through, there's nothing beneath his feet except a fall into a deep pit lined with stones, nothing left for him to do but circle restlessly and wait for the arrival of the howling dogs and the now silent men.

Alma snaps as many pictures as she can, ooohing and aaahing, but

Hannah, still sleepy-faced, just wants to return to her backseat nap, so after a few minutes we leave. Walking back to the car, I can't help thinking that this wolf trap is an *espectáculo cruél* as fixed as the bullfight I saw in Santarém a few days ago. Maybe, for the farm families I sat among, that bullfight mirrored the *cruél* but daily work necessary for a profitable farm, with just the right dab of danger to serve as a reminder of distant days when the beasties threatened your life and livelihood. Sure, the odds may be unfair, but that's how evolution works for the clever hungry ones at the top of the heap.

I can appreciate that. Alma and I have lived in small villages in Africa where the slope up to the food chain's tip is still slippery: spiders stretch wider than the span of a hand and scorpions bulk up to the size of lobsters, snakes subscribe to every poisonous persuasion and malaria can pack a fatal wallop, and the long white wire of a guinea worm will swell your leg to a log, while relentless rows of army ants march with their own collective ideas of what's what.

As we weave through Fafião on our way back home, Alma notices that some of these ancient stone houses have roofs that sport satellite dishes. I wouldn't mind parking and wandering about this village, but we have a long drive ahead of us, back to Viana do Castelo, where we've been indulging ourselves at a fancy *quinta*—country estate—that is perched on a steep hill.

The sun has worked its way down a good stretch of the sky by the time I steer past the estate's mansion and park in front of our stone-walled bungalow rental. Hannah, back from dreamland, feels refreshed enough for a romp in the outdoor pool, and within minutes we march, appropriately bathing-suited, through the manicured grounds. I can't help admiring how well this *quinta* is organized: above us, a series of terraces carved into the hill are laced with grapevines; one terraced level below, there's a grove for peacocks; and then we pass an enclosed pond with languidly circling swans. Stone steps lead us to a little plateau of a lawn, lined with rows of white-blossomed hydrangeas, and from there we can see the city below, clustered about the mouth of the Lima River as it meets the Atlantic Ocean, the Portuguese coastline curving into the hazy distance.

Alma decides the water in the pool is too cold, but Hannah and I judge it warm enough to plunge into. I shake off a shiver or two, then balance on one leg and lift the foot of the other just above the water—my version of a shark fin—and, hopping toward Hannah, I dumdumdum the music from *Jaws* until I'm splashed to defeat. Then we paddle toward the pool's far end, which has no raised concrete lip, so by keeping our heads at water level we prolong the thrilling illusion that we're floating toward the edge of a waterfall. Eventually, Hannah swims in her own circles, Alma pulls a lawn chair to poolside and pages through a book, and I float on my back, basking in the last of the day's sun. All those hours of driving melt away as, eyes closed, I let my thoughts wander, first over the trim surrounding lawn and the flower beds framing that spectacular view, then through the cloistered grounds for swans and peacocks, along the winding trails of cool stone steps, past the trellised grapevines, to our own cozy bungalow—so many examples of the cleverness of the human mind.

THREE CHURCHES

A huge banner runs down the length of the Church of Saint Stephen's white-stoned exterior, advertising a miracle that took place here 760 years ago. Over the centuries, kings and queens have visited this church in Santarém, a pedigree that only adds to the legend of the Shrine of the Most Holy Miracle. While Alma snaps a few photos, Hannah shades her eyes from the noonday sun. As for me, I'd much better appreciate the surrounding whitewashed buildings, their balconies lush with flowers, if I weren't still twitchy after navigating narrow cobblestone streets first designed when the internal-combustion engine was an impossible leap of imagination.

"Ready?" Alma asks, grinning. She still can't hide her pleasure at having found a website account of a miracle that goes back to 1247. A local woman, driven to despair by a philandering husband, consulted a sorceress in her cavern lair (only after the usual rosary prayers had gone unanswered), in the hopes that M-A-G-I-A might spell marital relief. The price? The unhappy wife merely had to supply a Communion wafer blessed by a priest and so transformed into the actual flesh and blood of Christ. Oh, how desperation in love can lead to uncharted territory.

During the following Sunday service, that determined wife, after receiving Communion, slipped the wafer from her mouth and bundled it into her veil, then scooted from the church. But a trail of bloody drops followed the woman on her way to the witch (waiting patiently in her cave outside of town), so she made a spooked beeline home instead and hid the bleeding wafer in a wooden chest. When her husband returned home late that night from his latest binge of someone else, great beams of blinding light shone through the planks of the trunk. Instantly terrified into fidelity, the husband knelt beside his wife and they prayed together until morning. The miracle wafer has been preserved in the church ever since.

When Alma first read this story, she knew that her unreconstructed-animist husband would want to come here. The local variety of spiritual quirks is yet another reason Portugal makes a cozy fit inside me. Even Lisbon newspapers are chockablock with classified ads that tout the services of African diviners from the former Portuguese colonies of Guinea and Angola, as well as more homegrown spiritualists. Our friend Fernanda only half-jokes when she tells us that unusual indeed is the Portuguese woman who hasn't consulted one of these guides. Alma once picked up from a *pastelaria* ladies' room the flier of a "consultora espiritual" boasting expertise in the subjects of love, sexual impotence, and *mal olhado*—the evil eye. More than once I've stood before the urinal of some Lisbon restaurant and read from a poster on the wall about the skills of Professor Sissé or Professor Ali, each well versed in the *segredos de magia negra ou branca*—secrets of black or white magic.

"Ready?" Alma repeats, and I nod, though I have to confess that my half-spoonful of unlapsed Catholic is just enough to fill me with a ripple of vestigial anxiety. Whenever I'm about to enter a church, I imagine my long absence might trigger an alarm.

No siren wails when we enter, just the roar of a huge death-to-all-dust vacuum pushed back and forth by an old woman in a corner of the modest interior: white walls, a geometric pattern of *azulejo* tiles, and a series of dark-hued paintings lining both sides of the church that depict the major plot turns of the miracle. But where's the magic wafer?

Alma approaches the old gal with the rumbling behemoth and gestures that she has a question. The woman frowns, fiddles with a switch, and the sudden silence almost hurts. While Alma warms up her latest informant, I take the opportunity to walk beneath the paintings and point out details to Hannah. "See there?" I say. "The wife is still in the church, but the wafer's already bleeding." And then, a few steps down, "And here's where she and her rotten husband are kneeling in front of the magical wafer." Hannah, who never indulged in the Harry Potter habit (preferring to gobble up the down-to-earth social dilemmas of tween novels), is only mildly interested in this spiritual drama.

Alma returns to report that the tabernacle housing the wafer is opened only during special religious holidays. Anticipating my disappointment, she has already picked up a devotional card from the souvenir stand in the back. One side of the card features a photo of a golden monstrance shaped like a sunburst, encircling a clear crystal where some gunk that once might have been a wafer is smeared with what once might have been dark blood. While Alma continues the tour of the paintings with Hannah, I stay behind and turn the card over to read a version of the story that's nearly identical to what Alma had read to me from the website. I'm about to set it aside when I notice a crucial difference: in this retelling, the scheming witch is a "Jewish sorceress."

I'd laugh out loud, but I'm too appalled. Though I'm not the kind of guy who willingly undermines someone else's religion, this particular miracle needs one big whopping asterisk. Unless you believe in transubstantiation—and *no* Jew believes in that—a Communion wafer is nothing more than a little cracker. Where's the motivation to steal one? So you can scratch the "Jewish" bit from the sorceress. But the kicker, and I think I speak with some authority here, is that no self-respecting Jewish girl would ever, *ever* live in a cave. Never happened, never will.

I feel as depressed as if I'd just uncovered a friend's awful, sleazy secret. At least someone felt guilty enough to scrub the slur from the website. And then I wonder, What happened to that so-called sorceress? I hope she didn't turn out to be some hapless scapegoat, providing dry-run fodder for the Inquisition looming two centuries down the line.

After her tour of the paintings, Alma sidles up beside me and says, "Pretty wild, huh?"

"Oh, you have no idea."

She gives me her *And so?* arched eyebrow, because my wife always knows when a juicy story is in the offing.

✳

We cut across the broad oval of the Rossio, Lisbon's popular *praça* lined with cafés catering to the tourist set, then linger for a moment before Peruvian musicians strumming guitars and tooting panpipes in front of the statue of Dom Pedro IV, until Hannah (who has discovered her shy self this year) whispers that I should drop a euro in the waiting guitar case. That contribution accomplished, we continue past a tiny hole-in-the-wall bar that serves *ginjinha*, a potent cherry liqueur that will, if you don't stop at one small glass, effect a secular version of transubstantiation by turning your legs into rubber.

Then we're standing before the Church of São Domingos. My asterisk to the miracle in Santarém has encouraged Alma to finally overcome her hesitancy about visiting this church, which holds an even grimmer story. In April 1506, the church was packed with people praying before a statue of the Virgin Mary, whose eyes appeared to be dripping tears. Perhaps the worshipers hoped this was a sign that the plague raging through the country might soon end. So when some New Christians—recent forcibly converted Jews— expressed doubts about the mechanics of the miracle, they were killed in the church aisles. The melee spread out into the Rossio and then throughout Lisbon, the mad three-day spree ending only after some two thousand Jews and New Christian converts had been killed. Decades later, the sentences of the Inquisition were announced in front of this church, just before the public roastings.

Again, no alarm goes off as I enter; instead, recorded voices of monks intoning Gregorian chants hover in the air. Which is a good idea, since in the absence of such calming music I might want to run from the place. Beneath the rose-colored curved ceiling, the church's stone pillars stand cracked and gouged, pieces missing—scars of the great Lisbon earthquake of 1755. Worse, the walls exude a faint scent of smoke, a lingering souvenir of a fire that ravaged São Domingos in the 1950s. If you were the sort to give God a mean-spirited street cred, you might say that he's taken revenge on this church.

A few worshipers sit in the wooden pews, but most stand toward the sides of the church, where a series of tables display little red cups holding stubby white candles, whose tiny flames flicker light to the dim surroundings. Hannah is immediately drawn to these candles, and when I explain that people light them in memory of loved ones who have passed away she nods at the need for this; all her grandparents are long gone, three before she was born, and their absence has always loomed large for her. Alma, as subdued as I've ever seen her, walks with Hannah to one of the tables, her hand already in her purse for the small change that bestows lighting privileges.

I stay behind and instead begin to make my way through the church as quickly as possible. The place contains too much of what chased me from the religion of my birth, its promise of peace mucked up with the mess of the world. I pass alcoves where statues of saints offer the standard devotional gaze, cross before the church's elaborate altar, and then stop, surprised.

Elevated halfway up a corner alcove and lit from above, a golden statue of the resurrected Christ seems to float in the air, his long robe draped over a body as lean as a Modigliani figure. His face bends down slightly with the gentle peace of a Buddha, and it seems that compassion could truly erase suffering. It's perhaps the calmest version of Jesus I've ever seen, and I feel I could stand here for hours—in *this* church, of all places—or at least long enough to reduce the heat on the bubbling stew beneath my mask of Everything's Okeydokey: my brooding and fits of anger, my need to please, and a self-pity that too easily shifts to self-importance.

Behind me, a woman sobs. I turn to watch her twisted face, framed by tangled, graying hair, as she lights a candle and ineffectually dabs at her eyes. Then she crosses the altar to weep before a statue of Jesus that's nestled in the opposite corner alcove—just released from the cross, he is cradled in his mother's arms, the sculpted marble realism of his dead body a landscape of pain and suffering that seems as far from the statue hovering above me as one could imagine. Why, I wonder, did she choose that Jesus? And why am I lingering *here*? I stare up again at my preferred version, and it hits me that Jesus is an ever-morphing all-purpose avatar. He's no longer himself—hasn't been, I guess, since the very beginning. If you want peace, then Jesus wants peace, too, but he's also not above underwriting fear, paranoia, or hatred, if you're so inclined. He's a chalice, waiting to be filled.

Before this visit, I thought I'd pegged how I would react, but the world holds its own mysteries, doesn't it? Down the length of this church, with its scars and scarred history, Alma still stands beside Hannah, who lights another candle, grateful for a chance to connect with relatives she's never met.

Sitting and waiting beside Alma in the vast interior of the Mosteiro dos Jerónimos, I can't quite believe this church managed to survive the earthquake of 1755 with nary a scratch. Its stone pillars, reaching to the heights of the intricately sculpted vault, appear far more delicate than they really are. The Portuguese, it seems, can work miracles with engineering skills in the service of the miraculous.

A thin, bald priest is halfway through intoning the Mass, with a voice so gentle and slow that I can understand most of his well-worn phrases of love and forgiveness, even as they echo in the enormous space of the church. Beside us sits Maria-José, a short woman with a wide, pleasant face that can shift from laughter to complaint and back again in an instant. The mother of Hannah's best friend Sara, she patiently endures our attempts to whisper chitchat in Portuguese during the occasional downtime of the Mass. In a few minutes, both girls will march to the altar and sing, as members of Os Pequenos Cantores de Belém, a children's chorus that performs in some of the classiest venues in Lisbon—they're even scheduled to record a couple of songs with a Portuguese opera star, Teresa Cardoso de Menezes. Hannah loves this chorus, even if rehearsals before a performance can stretch to four or more grueling hours. Alma, in perfect Jewish-mother mode, allows her pride in Hannah's voice and accomplishments to overlook the small detail of her daughter performing devotional songs in Latin.

While waiting, I glance about at the stained-glass windows, the endlessly rising pillars, and the church's entrance, where the tombs of Vasco da Gama and Luís de Camões lie side by side. They make a fitting pair, since Comões's epic poem *The Lusiads* glorifies da Gama's maritime discoveries, but if you ask me, the bones of the playwright Gil Vicente should spend their eternal rest here, too. Often compared to Shakespeare (who wrote nearly a century after him), Vicente wrote a trilogy of plays about life's end-game boats bound for heaven, hell, or purgatory that is a masterpiece of acid wit, stunningly skeptical about the corrupt underpinnings of Portugal's then still budding empire. Flip open to a page and you'll find an angel berating a nobleman who benefited from the country's then growing colonial holdings:

You despised lesser folk, looked down on them,
and as you grew prouder, became less than them

Flip to another page and there's the devil, accusing a cardinal of
emotional complicity in the crimes of the Inquisition:

Your *auto da fé*,
your act of faith,
was an act of hatred,
of a tortured soul
that knew only how to torture,
of twisted desire
that knew only
how to twist
and break.

Beats me how a fellow could write like that in the early sixteenth
century and still keep his head.

A side door opens, and the children walk in a line to the altar,
wearing dark-red robes topped with white collars. They settle into
two small groups on either side, like the separated wings of a bird.
Hannah and Sara stand together. On the opening day of that awful
first school Hannah briefly attended, she noticed Sara guiding a fellow student's wheelchair through the between-class chaos of the
hallway. From that moment their friendship began, and months
later the two girls, now in at least the shallows of adolescent sensitivity to the world's gaze, can still jostle and joke with each other like
kids. Sara's easy empathy is even more striking because she lived in
an orphanage until the age of ten, when Maria-José, a retired plastic
surgeon, adopted her. For the past two years, Sara's new mother has
been introducing her to the wider world.

Across the altar from Hannah and Sara stands the bully who so tor-
mented our daughter in that same first school. She's parked in the
other half of the chorus because, months ago, Hannah took the choral director aside and bravely requested that they be kept separated.
Though this girl (who we've heard once provoked her younger sister
to the point of writing a suicide note) has long since minded her p's
and q's, I still feel a flicker of rage at the sight of her.

Such a hard road, forgiveness.

The choral director raises her arms, holds them in the air, and when she nods the children's voices unfold a melody that balances somewhere between languid and stately. I close my eyes and try to make out the thread of my daughter's singing, and though a word, a phrase, seems to briefly hold her stamp I soon give in to the full blend of those young voices.

Each song seems flecked with something I can't exactly place, something beyond the Latin words of worship. Eventually I think I can hear, in the colors of those harmonies, the weaving back stories of Sara's orphanage, Hannah's challenging year, the bully's twisted talents, and even secrets of the other children that I know nothing about. Maybe that's what shapes this music's not quite tranquil beauty, the tangled stories these joined voices express and yet rise from, nearly untethered from trouble as the echoes in this vast church lift them just a little higher.

PARTICLE AND WAVE

"C'mon, please hurry up," I repeat as I knock on the door once more, attempting patience but failing. "You're going to be late." Hannah's spending more time than usual in the bathroom this morning—posing in outfit after outfit, giving her hair the once- and then twice-over for the occasion of her last day of school. Every detail must brush perfection, and let's not forget the careful, gliding application of perhaps too much lip gloss, and the trying on and off, and then on and off again, of an array of earrings. Minutes later, Alma knocks, then I follow, and finally our pleading pries our daughter, resplendent, out of the bathroom and the apartment.

Outside, we hurry up cobblestoned stairways, Hannah wearing her backpack, Alma and I lugging our laptops, and though we're walking just shy of a run my inner brakes are at the ready—after all these months of surviving a hair-raising anthology of Portuguese driving, today is no time to let down our guard. Hannah no longer tolerates any parental handholding, so Alma and I do our subtle best to sidle her between us as we skirt along the edge of the first roundabout, where cars speeding in circles are steered by pedal-to-the-metal commuters stoked on espresso and plotting the day's office politics.

We accomplish a quick street crossing and climb higher up the hill to a traffic blind spot at the corner of an apartment building, where the words "PARE PARA VER E SER VISTO"—Stop to See and Be Seen—are painted by the curb. Part of that warning is the outline of a little figure in full fling over the roof of a speeding car. I've dreamt about this doomed fellow, imagined my own upside-down spin through the air, and Alma's, and Hannah's.

Finally, we reach the second roundabout, whose grassy island is so long and wide that it includes a stand of trees and a statue, of Félix de Avelar Brotero, an eighteenth-century botanist who wrote several volumes on Portuguese plants. How apt, that a monument honoring a long-robed scholar clutching a book stands just a few steps from a school. Our last street to cross, named after the ophthalmologist Dr. Mário Moutinho, is equally apt, since 10 percent of the students attending Hannah's school are blind or suffer eye problems. The street's name could even double as an ironic comment on the clueless drivers zipping by—although signs cluster everywhere announcing the school's presence, the images of walking children might as well be stamped in invisible ink.

Before we step across this last street, I can't help myself and muster the word "Careful," despite Hannah's impatience with my worrying. Once, to her eternal dismay, I shouted at one spectacularly reckless driver, "Veja as crianças!"—my spontaneous try at "Watch out for the kids!" I would have knuckled the hood of his car if I'd been close enough.

After crossing the street intact, we stand at the edge of the school. Far from its gated entrance and the eyes of her friends, Hannah stops, accepts a goodbye kiss on her cheek with a frown, and then she's on her way. Alma and I have become, not quite overnight, embarrassments. We may have traveled to Portugal together, but recently our daughter has continued on ahead of us, into the land of adolescence.

We wait until she enters the school grounds, then make our way to the nearest bus stop. For the past few months, ever since the weather warmed up, Alma and I have wandered up and down Lisbon's hills, exploring new neighborhoods while taking breaks to work on a book we're writing together, a second volume about our long-ago lives in small African villages. Now that Hannah's school year is ending, this may be our last chance to enjoy this particular mix of work and pleasure, so for today I've picked out a circuit of some of our favorite haunts.

We run to catch the bus, which takes us on a short hop to the bottom of the Alto de Santo Amaro. From there, we climb the hill until we reach a small *praça* that's a buzzing local hub. One side of the shady square is lined with tables where old fellows (wearing an informal uniform of caps and faded button-down shirts) play cards while spectators wander from game to game, kids on bikes pop wheelies around the central fountain, and young mothers lounging on benches gossip beside baby strollers. Tables line the other side of this *praça*, too, but as these are rarely taken Alma and I almost always get our pick. We settle across from each other and pull out our laptops.

Alma tells me she's revising a scene of the ritual that renamed our son Nathaniel after a revered village ancestor, and she sighs once or twice as she tries to re-create our now twenty-year-old's then six-year-old self. Meanwhile, I'm writing about a madman: Matatu, the village's former barber. Soon after we first met him, when we had no idea what trouble he would cause himself and others, he stopped by our compound and drew out from a burlap bag all sorts of junk—an empty perfume bottle, a brown zipper—and claimed the items were treasures. They had to be, since he also announced, "Moi, je suis le prime ministre!"—Me, I'm the prime minister! One of the goodies in that sack was a small plywood box; a month later, I watched him hack it to tiny shreds with a broken scissors while singsonging "Denju, Denju," our son's African name.

After a couple of hours, our battery power dwindling, we pack up and haul ourselves down the hill to the bus stop for another hop—to Madragoa, a neighborhood whose layout of narrow winding streets predates the 1755 Lisbon earthquake. We stop at a tiny *tasca* whose closet-sized kitchen excels in moist and tender braised chicken. We sit, order red wine served in a ceramic jar, and try to ignore the little pug of a TV by the door. On the TV, a glossy chat show's cheery hosts entertain an easily entertained studio audience. Over our meal, Alma and I wonder what Hannah's doing right now on her school's lax last day, a day of parties and celebrations—playing foosball with Guilherme, or simply goofing it up with Patricia and the rest of the gang?

Later, we let our legs help us digest that hefty lunch. We hike down one avenue and then another, passing the occasional green *largo* or *praça*, always just a head-turn away from a breathtaking glimpse of the Tejo River, until we arrive at the Praça São Paulo and our favorite *pastelaria*. We'd first tried out this place on a whim, mainly because a free table near the wide window offered a clear view across the square.

It may seem like a typical *pastelaria*, compact and narrow, an espresso maker and a fresh-orange-juice machine parked behind the pastry counter, an array of liquor bottles lined against the mirrored wall, but the owners (a married couple whose accents mark them as Brazilian) attract the uninhibited and the down and out, maybe because they accept every strange turn of the day with good humor and patience. Our first time there, a woman entered the *pastelaria* and worked the tables, silently bestowing double-cheeked air-kiss hellos on each patron, though a flurry of sidelong glances made it clear that nobody knew her. When she started talking her own language of awkward mumbles, we all nodded until she finally finished expressing herself and, satisfied, went on her way.

Over our usual pot of tea and a silky *torta de laranja*, Alma and I plug in our computers and switch back to work while regulars sip tiny cups of espresso. A member of the Portuguese Association of Foreign Wars wanders from table to table, selling raffle tickets. In a corner, a gaunt old guy scratches the back of a fellow gaunt old guy, really getting into it. One table behind us, two Gypsy women take turns reading the palm of a man so drunk he keeps forgetting what they tell him, so they roll out one do-over after another until he snags four or five fortunes. Then he wobbles out to the sidewalk, off to his new multibranched future.

I'm not sure what scene Alma is writing now, but I'm still working on Matatu. The creepy, quiet insistence of the man and the havoc he wrought still give me chills, and I can see him as he teased more treasures from his sack, an empty matchbox, a ball of tinfoil, a dusty cassette without a case. "C'est jolie, n'est-ce pas?"—It's lovely, isn't it?—he kept asking, and I found myself responding, "Oui, c'est jolie," the two of us, with only words, creating beauty out of garbage.

I'm almost through my first draft of the scene when I hear the rounded tones of West African French spoken behind me. Stunned, I turn to see a man poised before the counter, his lean, dark face wracked with sadness. He's telling the owners that *he* is the boss. "Je suis le patron!" he repeats, shaking from some secret passion. He's there before us and yet somewhere else, too, and the owners understand this and manage to lead him gently out the door.

Alma's blanched face must surely reflect my own, because this is more than a couple steps beyond eerie. When a coincidence comes my way, sometimes it's simply a minor triumph of chance, but a coincidence can also offer a lucky opportunity. This time, I grab what has been given, realizing that Matatu, frightening as he may have been, was also a suffering soul, whose misery had so soaked into his life that there was no wringing it out—important for me to remember as I apply a version of him onto the page.

I putter away at a few more sentences, but soon it's time to return to Hannah's school and we head for the nearest bus stop. A sun shower sweeps in; Alma, ever prepared, produces an umbrella from some inner pocket of her computer bag, and we share it as we stand outside the crowded glass shelter, share the typical bus-stop pause, when there's nothing much to do except wait. There's an absent smile on Alma's lips, and her large, dark eyes glisten, seem to be gazing at some private vista, but then she focuses on me, that smile remaining. As usual, I feel unworthy yet grateful, remembering my favorite lines from a poem by Pedro Tamen: "When you don't speak, you speak, and you know / the words I say and don't say." We're in one of those moments that are worth all the work of marriage, a moment to linger over, but there's the bus, huffing around a corner. We line up with our monthly passes in hand.

The Portuguese can be a quiet bunch on a bus, nurturing individual invisible thought bubbles. Alma likes to say they're a nation of daydreamers. She prefers to rewind the day's events as she sits beside me, and she does so until she catches on that I've stopped responding. I'm a dreamer, too. I prefer my own quiet as the grunting of the engine and the rattling of the bus windows become distant background music to the passing city. Block after block, the sight of newspaper kiosks reminds me I forgot to buy a paper today, reminds me of the challenge I set myself whenever I approach a newsstand: standing a few feet away, I'll silently repeat the polished phrases I've worked out word by word, hoping to mimic the local accent. This little game derives from my fragile wish to sustain, if only for a moment, the illusion that I'm Portuguese, though I really can't say why, since I do and don't feel at home here—just as a particle becomes a wave function becomes a particle becomes a wave, I oscillate between comfort and unease. And anyway, the odds are tipped against me, because after nearly a year I'm still stalled at the "Me Tarzan, you Jane" stage of language proficiency.

Sure, I can survive a chat at the grocer's or the butcher shop, and, yes, I've memorized the spoken rituals of ordering at a restaurant. I can even catch the gist of the local TV news if I know the context, and I manage to stumble through the newspaper each day, though there always comes that awful moment when I grasp every word in a sentence and still have no clue how it all adds up. I've puzzled through my pocket dictionary so often all the pages have ragged edges, and still the language eludes me. My friend Luís once mentioned that a certain internal resistance needs to be overcome before one can submit to the logic of another language. If only I could locate that crucial wall, I'd jackhammer it to smithereens.

"Here we are," Alma says, popping my thought bubble as the bus idles in front of Hannah's school. We step off, enter through the gate, and at once feel the crackle in the air of the whole wide summer waiting. The cobblestoned courtyard, dotted with palm trees, nearly bursts with a jumble of students. Grade-schoolers chase each other around clusters of very grown-up ninth-graders itchy to graduate, and Alma and I try to pick out Hannah in the crowds.

There she is, circled by classmates trading hugs and smooches on the cheek, and she chatters away in a Portuguese as idiomatic as theirs. Skinnied down to Portuguese-girl proportions, her arms covered with heartfelt expressions of friendship written by her pals in pen, Hannah appears to have achieved a seamless acceptance. Her favorite teacher, Professora Robalo, stands teary-eyed beside her, and after Alma takes one more photo than Hannah can tolerate we say *adeus* with kisses and handshakes and long, lingering waves.

Beginning our return round of traffic cat-and-mouse with our walking yearbook of a daughter, we pause by the curb while I stare down a driver who slowed for the crosswalk only at the last grudging second. I like the daydreaming Portuguese when they're sitting in a bus much more than when they're behind the wheel of a car. When we're halfway across the first roundabout, Alma tries convincing Hannah to return to school later in the evening for a scheduled year-end bash, but she shakes her head no. "Why not?" Alma asks. Hannah, staring straight ahead, finally explains, "I don't think I can handle saying goodbye a second time."

Something in her voice pulls the blinders from my pride in what she has accomplished this year. She didn't ask to come here. We dragged her from friends in Illinois, and now, after carefully constructing new friendships out of her daily progress in the language, word by phrase by conjugation, she'll soon have to leave them behind, too. Who knows when they'll ever meet again? As we stand once more at the corner where that little figure destined for the emergency room lies painted on the street, I decide to distract Hannah from her sadness by showing off my Googling skills. Pointing at the sign labeled RUA GREGÓRIO LOPES, PINTOR DO SÉCULO XVI, I say, "The Portuguese know how to do things right, naming a street for an artist. Lopes was one of the local big shots of the Renaissance. He painted the *Martyrdom of Saint Sebastian*; you know, that guy with all the arrows in him—"

When Hannah flashes me a look I can only describe as aggressive boredom, I realize I've entered Annoying Dad territory, but it's too late to stop me: I have more than one bone to pick with the next street, Rua Antão Gonçalves, Navegador do Século XV. Taking part in the great explorations initiated by Prince Henry the Navigator, Gonçalves was the first modern European to buy Africans and transport them as slaves to Europe. Not the sort of fellow who deserves *any* street, much less one that curves alongside a high school and a community swimming pool. "Jeez," I grouse, "couldn't they have given him a blind alley leading to a toxic-waste dump instead?"

We make a right turn at the dry cleaner's and walk down Rua Diogo de Silves, named after another explorer from the fifteenth century, one far more worthy of his stretch of pavement. *He* discovered the Azores, those gloriously green islands in the middle of the Atlantic, and I remind our silent daughter of the dreamy vacation we spent there a few years back.

Down cobblestoned steps we descend, until finally we're back at our apartment on Rua Alberto Villaverde Cabral, named after a journalist. Before I can get started on that Hannah hurries away to her room, the door shutting behind her. She's off to IM her friends back home, or maybe she'll add to one of the stories and poems she's filled her notebooks and computer folders with all year. Alma already sits ensconced on the couch with the phone book, searching for the best shipping company—in a few weeks, we'll slowly strip our apartment down to its original self, as it was before we first arrived. In prenostalgic mode, I pull back the living-room curtains for a glimpse of the sliver of the Tejo River visible from our window, and there at the end of the street is the tiny park named after Fernanda de Castro, a twentieth-century poet who also wrote plays and translated Rilke and Pirandello into Portuguese.

I've always been tickled that our street and that bordering park are named after writers, though truly it's not unusual. Lisbon is dotted with streets and parks and statues honoring novelists and poets, and the most obscure literary prizes are celebrated in the newspapers. Even months later, I can't get over how, when the surrealist poet and painter Mário Cesariny died, every Lisbon daily spread his photo across the front page, and most devoted at least their next six pages to his life and work. When it comes to writers, the Portuguese indeed know how to do it right. I think I know why. With so much of the national identity based on great feats of exploration in the distant past, writers are the ones who mainly continue this tradition, though they're plucky, patient explorers of a different sort, discovering interior empires.

That little park named after Fernanda de Castro is neatly landscaped, with a few willow trees casting shade over benches that sometimes host subdued lovers or a single lone soul. Standing by the window, with Alma turning pages behind me, I can imagine slipping outside to sit beneath those willows. Who knows? On the eve of our leaving, with a notebook on my lap, my head bent in thought, and my own Portuguese cap perched on my head, I just might be taken for someone who actually belongs there.

FAIRLY MEDIEVAL

After only a few steps inside the castle gate, Hannah and Sara clutch each other in mock horror as a ragged beggar shuffles by, his cheeks, arms, and legs dotted with impressively realistic rubber boils and pus-filled wounds. The girls may giggle at this make-believe, but a nervous edge to their voices suggests they'd rather not encounter another guy like this just yet, so Alma and I lead them up a nearby stack of broad stone steps, to the top of the castle wall.

Once there, we amble along the ramparts to take in the town of Óbidos below: the multiple geometries of angled red tiled roofs, almost impossibly whiter-than-white buildings, and great swathes of red and purple flowers, all tucked into the oval expanse of ancient stone walls. In the distance loom higher walls protecting the castle keep, that last line of defense when all else is lost. We might as well be a million miles from the wind turbine farms we drove past on our way here an hour ago—one hundred or so sleek and towering windmills, their enormous white blades turning slowly in the bluest sky.

The cobblestone streets below are Disney theme park–thick with visitors to the town's annual summertime medieval fair. Óbidos, though, has Mickey & Co. beat by a millennium and then some. This town, which goes back to Roman times, has seen Visigoths and Muslims come and go. Then, in 1220, King Afonso II gave Óbidos to his princess bride as a wedding present, and every king since has followed that romantic and rather high-handed gesture. I can see why—the town is a buffed-up version of what any royal couple might fondly imagine the rest of their country looks like.

Hannah and Sara peek through the ordered gaps in the top of the walls, out at the green countryside stretching away, and then pull back with muted happy shrieks, as if dodging incoming arrows. The girls bring out the joy in each other, and I wonder if they're so close because much of the world is still new to Sara, who lived in an orphanage until she was ten, while all of Portugal is new to Hannah.

Alma's cell phone bleeps—it's our friend Helena, calling to say she and her friends are running about an hour late. So we decide to buy our tickets and enter the castle keep, where most of the fair takes place. Soon we're walking through narrow alleys of tents filled with medieval kitsch, jewelry, leatherwork, jars of local honey, fresh bread, and flagons of wine, all peddled by hawkers decked out in full reenactment mode—leather vests and felt caps, shawls and tunics. A Gypsy offers palm readings, and Alma, who's wanted a crack at one of these all year, enters the tent. While we wait, Sara and Hannah hurry off to buy each other little matching gifts, avowals of undying friendship, since they have only two weeks left to spend together.

Alma emerges a few minutes later with a mysterious wouldn't-you-like-to-know look on her face. We continue past an enormous pig turning on a spit, its fat crackling as it roasts, then past smithies clanging away, one grimy fellow pulling and pushing a huge bellows. I used to play with toy castles when I was a kid (one is still boxed up in the basement back home), and now I feel as if I've shrunk down to the size of my old figurines of knights, squires, and peasants while they have somehow come to life. Then an executioner, shouldering an ax, makes his way through a crowd that easily parts before him. He doesn't notice anyone, however; his eyes look inward, and when he lets out a high-pitched giggle I'm back in this century, relieved not to be living in another.

Two or three combos of big drums, bagpipes, and narrow-stemmed horns wander through the keep, playing a frenetic music that, if you listen too closely, can set your legs to jitters. We stroll past booths displaying broad leather belts and herbal sachets, and then we come upon a young woman who furtively glances back and forth beneath her scarf as she hunches by, pulling at a long string tied around a triangular stone, leading it as though it were a pet. A gray-haired crone (well, someone twenty-something sporting a wig and penciled-in wrinkles) follows her, exuding disapproval. They seem attached by their own invisible string, a mother accompanying her grown child's skittish mad path.

We come to a small stage where belly dancers, midriffs bared, draped in jewelry and strings of bells, click their hand cymbals and swirl gauzy veils with a slink and a swoop to three musicians' flute, drum, and tambourine stylings. Hannah and Sara can't stop staring at all those silky moves, so we watch until Alma gets another call— Helena and company have finally arrived. We make our way out of the keep, but not before our palms are stamped so we can return.

As we enter the courtyard outside the gate, dark-haired Helena waves, flanked by Jorge, her lanky handsome boyfriend, and her best friend, pale and delicate Sónia, along with a handful of their wider circle of friends. This past year we've joined the group on hikes through the sprawling Monsanto Park overlooking Lisbon; to an underground excavation of the ancient Roman version of the city; to a vegetarian feast at a Tibetan restaurant; and now we double-kiss, shake hands, and embrace with a sad edge—today may be the last time we see each other before leaving.

While we're all chatting away, one of the belly dancers from the keep saunters by and calls out Helena's name. They hug and kiss, and it turns out, once introductions are made, that this dancer's day job in the twenty-first century is conducting research at a biochemistry lab.

It figures. Most of Helena's circle is pushing thirty or beyond, and they're among the cream of the crop of Portugal's first post-Salazar generation, yet sometimes they have to live from government research grant to research grant or make do with temporary jobs out of town. Newspaper articles describe the plight of bank tellers and store clerks with degrees in sociology or journalism who struggle at the end of each month. Helena, an accomplished forestry biologist, is considering a research job in Aveiro, one that might eventually offer her more security, even though her boyfriend Jorge, a botanist, has just returned to Lisbon from a six-month gig in Castelo Branco near the Spanish border. Sónia's work with endangered wolves doesn't get her much more than a small apartment, Joel has an economics degree but survives by writing reviews of the latest cameras while winning awards for his own photos, and Joana, a bioengineer, has found better employment in the United States. They're as talented a group of folks as I've ever met: multilingual, juggling professional careers with artistic pursuits—music, photography, poetry (and, apparently, belly dancing)—yet somehow the country still hasn't figured out how to unleash and reward the energies of this generation. We retrace our steps through the keep with Helena and the gang, pass a group of knights lazing about after a joust we just missed, do a little more idle shopping, stand for a while around one of the bands making a mesmerizing racket. Everyone's getting hungry, so we make our way to a huge outdoor grill, where strips of beef, chops, and sausages sizzle side by side. Traditional soups are on offer—*sopa da pedra*, *açorda*, and local delicacies like *migas*, a gooey mix of bread, garlic, bits of pork, and cilantro that I can't get enough of. And let's not forget the inviting drinks served in brown ceramic cups, such as Elixer da Juventude (Youth's Potion) and Sangue de Boi (Ox Blood) and Levanta Mortos (Raise the Dead).

We take our plates and cups to the stone steps of a nearby outdoor amphitheater that extends up a gentle slope, stopping short of the castle walls, and we commandeer front-row seats before an empty stage. But something's in the works, because soon a thousand or more people slowly fill the curve of the amphitheater behind us: *avós* and *avôs*—grandmothers and grandfathers—young families, couples, even babies in strollers.

A comedy troupe takes the stage to prove that vaudeville's ancestry didn't begin in the Catskills, that slapstick joshing, juggling, basic magic tricks, and pratfalls probably predate the invention of the wheel. Hannah sits beside Sara and, beset by another stomach ache, merely nibbles at her meal, while Alma bends her head in deep conversation with Helena, calculating the plusses and minuses of moving to Aveiro. Feeling restless, I get up to stretch my legs and make my way to a corner that looks out over the rest of the keep as the evening deepens into night, the distant lights of nearby towns small points in the darkness. From now on, our last two weeks will be packing, packing, packing, punctuated by more than a few misty-eyed farewells. I can't help regretting that we never took a boat ride up the Douro River to view the vineyards, or explored the wild northern corner of Trás-os-Montes. I could stretch this list, but what's the point, this unseemly urge to linger? Hannah, despite her deepening friendship with Sara, is antsy to return to her school friends back home.

A handful of young men dressed as squires (who might actually be medical interns) pass by, pulling the carriage of some faux noblewoman (who could be a law clerk) peeking out of a circular window, and I'm surprised that even this late the reenactors keep themselves busy, that drums still rumble beneath plaintive bagpipes. When I notice a juggler off in a quiet corner, performing for no one but his own self beneath a tree, I wonder why they're all so reluctant to abandon the playacting—there must be some stronger draw than part-time fun for a little extra cash.

The executioner with his creepy giggle walks past me, and I decide to return to the amphitheater. The slapstick performers are gone, the ancient walls of the castle are now lit from within, and all those roving bands have converged on the stage, the big sound of their joined forces threatening an out-of-the-body lift.

We turn to the surprise of shouts and gasps behind us: along the grassy verge beneath the castle walls, skulking gray-skinned fallen angels and horned devils wrapped in scraps of animal fur have lit torches. To booming drums they march down, parting the audience on their way to the stage. The musicians continue to play but slip to the side, giving way to these figures waving fiery arcs, who then give way to bare-chested men dancing on stilts, the bottoms of those long wooden legs blazing with fire. Then two women take their place, swinging over their heads what look like giant bat wings, though these shower sparks and flames, until six woman arrive swinging pots of fire in circles, their faces eerily expressionless. The whole spellbinding panoply rages on and on, drums chasing multiple rhythms, bagpipes spinning a tumble of notes like berserker music, a trancelike call to overwhelm some enemy that will be real sorry, real soon.

Maybe it's the light and shadows cast by these swinging flames on the rapt faces of the audience, but it seems to me that everyone sitting around us is digging deep into the wildest part of their Portuguese soul, back to the time before the taming church, before the Islamic control of Iberia, to the steely core that eventually battled back the country, the essential inner itch that then set Portugal to building ships that sailed off into the frightening vastness of all the uncharted waters of the world.

The music stops in midphrase, a flourish of silence after the last notes echo against castle walls. We all give ourselves a little mental shake, stand, and start to make our way out of the keep. Hannah and Sara have the wilted look of a too-long day, so Alma and I decide we'll search out some nearby *pensão* for the night. First we linger a while with Helena and Jorge, Sónia and the rest, not quite ready to say goodbye. But say goodbye we do, then watch our friends blend into the departing crowds, off to their cars and the long drive back to Lisbon, back to the present time of frustrating job searches, where their tiny apartments can barely contain the raucous buzz of this evening they'll bring home.

GOODBYE, GOOD LUCK

With small steps we stop and start, following a long, winding customs line at JFK Airport. Before us, high walls display folk-art murals of America's multicultural bragging rights, a best face forward that's conveniently short on the bruises, scars, and broken teeth of our country's growing pains. I almost make a crack about this, but Alma and Hannah look as beat as I feel from our long day's travel, so I don't ruffle the silence. We still have ahead of us a cab ride to the car rental office, an hour's drive upstate to a hotel near Nathaniel and Emily's college campus, and then a too short night of sleep before we all meet the next morning, so I calculate times and distances and divide them by our collective exhaustion, and suddenly it's our turn to present passports.

The officer in the booth slides Alma's passport through a slot, glances at a computer screen, and nods, and he does the same with Hannah's. With mine, though, he stares at the screen, taps at a keyboard, stares again, this time with a frown, and types again. I don't like the look of that frown, and I'm only half surprised when he stands up and says, "Sir, you'll have to come with me."

"Um, why, what's the matter?"

"I'm not authorized to say. Follow me, please."

This is not, I'm sure, an invitation to a special welcoming party complete with balloon animals and cake. I nod and follow, immediately a Suspicious Figure to the people in line behind us, and I try to affect a bemused *Who, me?* expression. Alma draws out a nervous version of her admirable efficiency and peppers the fellow's Guilty-until-Proven-Innocent silence with questions. Hannah grabs my hand, as if this will help contain her delight—I can tell she's already planning to regale her friends with the juicy details of how I somehow get out of this scrape that I've gotten myself into.

In a corner back room run by the New York City Police, an officer behind a long desk squirms his mouth into an embarrassed smile as he questions out of me the sorts of personal tidbits that only I should know. Then there's more of that frowning at a computer screen I can't see, and the officer tells me my answers will be sent to the State Department in Washington, where some curious official will determine, in an hour or so, who I really am. Hey, I decide not to say, I've been trying to figure that out for years.

Though Alma insists on staying with me, I remind her of our one hundred tons of baggage that will soon be circling the carousel. "But please," I say, lowering my voice after a quick glance at Hannah, "don't let her do too much—ask someone to help, OK?" Alma nods and looks away, and before they leave I kiss my daughter on the forehead and force a grin. "This won't take too long, kiddo. Really."

After settling down in a chair, I return to the airplane-friendly novel I'd been plowing through over the Atlantic, a sci-fi bust-up set in mid-twenty-first-century India. Meanwhile, busywork continues at the front desk: officers scan computer screens, joke about a recent fishing trip, and occasionally call up for questioning subdued families or individuals who look as if they've recently arrived from the currently suspicious neighborhoods of Dubai, Syria, or Pakistan. Behind me, a dog revs up some impressive whimpering, and I glance back at two dark-haired guys conferring in whispers beside a carrying case pocked with air holes.

An hour ticks away, and as artificial intelligence entities shaped as Hindu gods streak through the walls of the future, I can't help bookmarking page after page with worry. Where are Alma and Hannah waiting, and what might be running through their minds as I'm stuck here with no stateside cell phone to call them? Is this little interlude a case of identity theft or something more sinister? Sticking my paranoia on a hook and casting it out to deep waters, I imagine some Junior Dick Cheney squinting over his glasses at my secret file, reading a satirical piece I recently published about the Bush administration's petitioning to have waterboarding declared an Olympic sport. Or maybe he's taking notes on the piece that blames the administration's astonishing incompetence on a secret purchase of the entire catalog of dicey Acme products from Looney Tunes. And then there's that dispatch I wrote comparing Bush to the Portuguese dictator Salazar . . . well, if that's what they're up to, I'll sue 'em, *sue 'em*, I have First Amendment rights, I have—

In the middle of this self-righteous tear, I hear those two guys with the dog worrying out loud in Portuguese, and though it's the open-voweled Brazilian variety, I'm still shocked at this unexpected final wave goodbye from the language that surrounded me for a year. Hannah wouldn't be impressed. A firm fan of the European Portuguese she's learned, she sometimes mocks the Brazilian pronunciation of *tarde*—afternoon—and *grande*—big. "TAR-jeeee, GRAN-jeeee," she'll grimace, preferring the "tar-deh" and "gran-deh" of her thin thin school friends, who during our last Lisbon days trooped to our apartment to visit our popular daughter while Alma and I arranged the chaos of our living room into suitcases.

Off-target accent or not, the sound of Portuguese dings a neglected synapse: I forgot to eat the fig I'd placed on a plate in our otherwise empty refrigerator. Weeks ago, I'd first plotted out a little ritual of farewell: a solitary fig would await me on our last morning, to be enjoyed in the minutes before a taxi arrived to drive us to the airport. I'd imagined that this plump, succulent fruit would somehow hold the taste of our time in Lisbon. Now I suspect I forgot to follow through this morning because I no longer want to savor this past year.

By now, two hours have passed and the Brazilians are long gone, their sorry visaless selves sent back home, while those folks of seemingly every Middle Eastern persuasion have been allowed to continue on their innocent way. "Mr. Graham?" the young officer finally calls out from behind the long desk. When I approach he says, "You're OK to go, you're in the clear."

That's it? Goodbye and good luck, as if nothing ever happened? "Excuse me," I ask, "but can you tell me what this was all about?"

He hesitates, not sure how many beans to spill, if any, and then I'm offered, in a This-Is-Just-Between-Us voice, "Let's say there's a bad guy out there with a name that's close to yours."

Oh really, I grump to myself as I head for the baggage claim area, could there actually be some terror-coded fiend out there in the wider world named Osama Phil Graham? When I finally locate the correct carousel, there sit Alma and Hannah's forlorn figures on the edge of our mounds of baggage—castaways stranded on the shore of Suitcase Island, population, two. They both rise, relieved to see me, but before the first of Alma's million questions can leave her lips, Hannah says, "Look, Dad, I helped pull all those bags," and I stare as she flexes an imaginary muscle on an impossibly thin arm. She looks nine or ten, not twelve—as if our child has reversed time, back to before we ever lived in Lisbon.

*

The train glides along the tracks on this first leg of our day trip down to New York City, Hannah tucked snugly between Alma and me as we sit across from Nathaniel and Emily, surrounded by the unaccustomed soundscape of spoken English—the conductor's call for tickets at each stop, the fleeting chatter of new passengers in the aisles. Yet none of us are talking, as if we don't know quite what to say, and maybe that's why Hannah starts a Portuguese word game she learned in school. On a piece of paper she works up the required chart that will soon be filled with categories of words we'll have to guess. Nathaniel and Emily are granted the rights of English, while Alma and I join Hannah in trolling for the correct Portuguese answers.

Our game catches the attention of a family sitting across the aisle from us—a young couple and their daughter, who looks to be about six or seven. "Bom Dia,"—Good morning—the man says, though it comes out as bom-*jeee*-a, the mark of a Brazilian. We get a conversation going and tell our tale, and then it turns out that the father has recently arrived here to study for a year in the United States, and their daughter will attend an American public school and learn English. Once this sinks in we stare: our two families could be mirror images of each other.

Another of those coincidences offering opportunity has swooped down, and Alma and Hannah are already on it—they cross the aisle and squeeze in beside the family. Hannah's fluid Portuguese, a single year in the making, seems enough to reassure the girl and her parents, and Alma offers tip after tip about New York and culture shock. I stay put beside Nathaniel and Emily, and when he leans across to her and marvels, "This sort of thing happens *all the time* in my family,"

I half-join our usual joshing, though I can't shake the feeling that I'm being stalked by the invisible seams of the universe.

That child's gaze won't leave Hannah. There's more to this than a younger girl's awe of an older girl. I recognize that lost look in her eyes, tethered as she is to this strange new world only through her parents—a look of veiled vulnerability that reminds me of Hannah during those first weeks of Lisbon. Why couldn't I have seen it then as clearly as I do now?

When our train pulls into Grand Central Station, we all stand and stretch and make our way out to the platform and exchange farewells. I lead the father a step or two to the side and say, "Adeus, boa sorte"— Goodbye, good luck—and he replies in English, "Thank you," and I want to tell him about Hannah's year of isolation from her friends back home and the absurd challenge of placing her in a Portuguese school, and how the miseries of that first, frightful school remained raw and stinging; how she was so desperate to fit in at her second school that she crash-coursed the Portuguese language, brilliantly, but she also wanted, *needed*, to look like her skinny new friends, so she dieted—first openly and then secretly—down to their size, her stomachaches actually hunger pangs, and during our last days in Lisbon it became clear that she doesn't know how to stop; I want to tell him that we're traveling to Chinatown in the hopes of tempting Hannah away from this path with a feast of her favorite dim sum treats, hoping to unvanish our vanishing child; I want to warn him to take care of his daughter, to understand the trials of language immersion that she'll face in a school far, far from home; I want to tell him to be mindful of his child's moods and be worthy of her secrets, and above all to love her, to love her fiercely, and better yet to go back home, go back home *now*, now while you can, *go home now*.

I stand there, these words unborn on my half-pursed lips, because I can't yet face the seriousness of what might lie ahead for our child or for us, because I'm afraid that if I speak these words aloud our worst fears might come true. This father pauses, not sure if he's misread my intent to speak. Our eyes have locked for a fraction too long. Yet still I stand there, silent, knowing I can't step up to what the coincidence of our meeting asks of me, knowing how much I'll regret my failure to warn him away from my mistakes.

He half-shrugs, turns, and joins his wife and child.

Mere seconds have passed by. My own family hasn't noticed any pause. With a few steps—weighted with self-loathing—I've joined them, and we walk together on the platform, continuing our quest to Chinatown. Already we've lost sight of that nice young Brazilian family in the hustling crowds ahead.

SIₚ BY SIₚ

I open the steamer cover and there rest two plump chicken breasts, ready for spearing. I plop them onto the cutting board and slice into the white, stringy meat, checking to make sure each piece is cooked through and through before chopping it into smaller pieces. Transferring this mound of diced chicken to the blender, I avert my eyes from the narrow band of Portuguese tiles that spans the walls of our kitchen, a coiling floral pattern of blue, white and yellow. Alma and I bought these *azulejos* years ago during a first, brief vacation to Lisbon, then remodeled the kitchen around them. Right now I'd rather not be reminded.

Our daughter, led by an inner voice of terrible discipline that whispers siren songs of subtraction, has crossed a dangerous invisible line. Since our last days in Lisbon she hasn't accepted more than a morsel to eat, and now, nearly a month back home, Alma and I have long passed worry and are firmly in fright. So I'm turning my fear to meticulous detail: into the blender go the chicken chunks, then splash after splash of stock before I press frappé, and after the blender fills with a pasty chicken mush I pour it all into a pot on the stove, along with two cans of navy beans. Solid food may be impossible for Hannah to even consider, but soup might work, a soup that is secretly solid, and Alma is helping keep that secret by distracting Hannah upstairs, so she won't come down and see what I'm up to.

She won't touch this if it's called chicken soup, so "vegetable soup" it will have to be, and I open the refrigerator door in search of the usual suspects. Hannah loved the soups of Eurizanda, our versatile housecleaner back in Lisbon, who gave Alma lessons in Cape Verdean creole while teaching me how to repair a leaky bathroom pipe with a line of string and a dab of elbow grease. Once a week Eurizanda cooked a huge pot of creamy vegetable soup for us, thick with a deep orange glow that proclaimed her preference for carrots, and she gave each simmering gift a little extra oomph, knowing that whenever Hannah returned home from school to a new soup's inviting smell, she'd beg for a bowl before the front door could close behind her.

Rarely will you be served a simple plate of vegetables anywhere in Portugal, yet our small local grocery in Lisbon sported so much fresh produce, in bins overflowing with squashes and leafy greens of all sorts, that Alma and often I wondered, Where do all those veggies go? Eventually, Eurizanda's savory offerings clued us in that, in Lisbon and across the country, they disappeared into onion soups and pumpkin soups and carrot and green bean and kale soups. Of course, the Portuguese being Portuguese, in every bowl lurked a chunk of ham, or an egg, or recycled stale bread—or now, in my case, enough protein to legally declare this soup a living thing.

So I proceed through the tedious task of disguise by peeling clove after clove of garlic; dividing potatoes into halves, quarters, eighths; slicing onions at both ends before pulling back the brown crinkly skin to begin chopping; plucking stubby green flowers of broccoli from thick stems until they lie across the cutting board like a tiny devastated forest. All is flung into the waiting pot, along with a bag of diced carrots, no—two bags, then another, to get that proper orange glow.

Eurizanda isn't the only presence hovering over these anxious tweakings. As I heat the burner and begin stirring, I'm also haunted by my last meeting with Grace Paley, my college writing mentor who passed away in late August, only two weeks ago. Last June, not long before the end of our Lisbon stay, I flew to the States to teach a brief graduate writing workshop at Vermont College, my first time back home in nearly a year. While there an old friend, the poet Jean Valentine, told me she'd heard that Grace had taken a bad turn in a fight against cancer. Grace lived only thirty miles away, so Jean and I drove a rental car through Vermont's lush green summer landscape to visit her, and after the last stretch of a narrow road cutting through a field or two and then a stand of thick overhanging trees, we came to her front yard, where she sat beside a table, waiting for us.

She looked like an older version of the Grace I'd always known, her classic topknot now wispy white hair crowning her head. After careful hugs of greeting, Jean and I joined Grace, her husband Bob, and their stunning daily view: great lazy rolls of cloud that crossed a blue sky and cast shadows on the hills below. Though she could forget something just five minutes past, Grace still had her clear-eyed humor, sharp and gentle at the same time. She landed some tough ones on Bob, but he joked off the rough edges and she seemed to expect this, because it was all an improvised show of a crusty, loving couple.

We skimmed along on friendly chitchat, nothing approaching what I was too embarrassed to say, that Grace, by the example of her patient teaching, the clarity and heart of her writing, even a single sentence from one of her stories—"Everyone, real or invented, deserves the open destiny of life"—had given me a way to live my own life, given me a path I'd tried, however imperfectly, to follow.

At a scurry of steps above me, I pause in mid-stir. Scanning the cutting board and countertop, I reach for and then toss an offending empty can of beans into the garbage. I listen for steps down the stairs but none come. However she managed it, Alma has done her job. So I continue stirring and return to the moment when Grace invited us to stay for dinner and Jean and I exchanged alarmed glances—we hadn't come to impose. But Bob led me to the family garden, where we gathered greens. He and I carried it all to the kitchen while Jean kept Grace company. Bob found a box of pasta, I chopped vegetables, then poked around in the refrigerator for ingredients that might work together with spaghetti sauce. Not much there, and a good proportion of that was too old to use—this was the kitchen of a family under siege.

When Grace called Bob to the front yard, he turned to me and I said, "Don't worry, I'll take over." Suddenly there I stood, alone in the kitchen, with two pans simmering. Somehow, step by tiny step I had been given this opportunity to offer my mentor a meal. The spaghetti sauce now seemed unworthy, so I searched the cabinets and scoured through the refrigerator once again, hoping for any spice or condiment that might help match the depth of my gratitude.

I steamed the greens and then shaped them into a kind of loaf, grilled some garlic bread, simmered the sauce until it poured thick over the steaming spaghetti, and I called everyone in to the table I'd just set. Bob scarfed down his portion with exaggerated praise— glad, I guessed, to eat a meal he hadn't prepared himself, though more likely he was trying to encourage Grace, her appetite hijacked by cancer. When Jean joined in with compliments intended as gentle nudging, Grace managed a bite or two, and I wondered if she could taste what my meal was trying to say.

By now today's soup is bubbling nicely before me, and I add more chicken stock, a pinch of salt and pepper, then dip in a hand blender until the chunky mix smoothes to an even texture. When the time comes, I'll slip into Hannah's portion a tab or two of butter, a brimming tablespoon of olive oil, and as much heavy cream as I can get away with. But Grace and Eurizanda are the essential seasonings, the understanding that all food must contain the invisible, transformative spice of love. Even a small cup, a single spoonful of this soup will be a secret feast. That's how we will do this. That's how Hannah will return to us. Sip by sip.

ON THIS SIDE OF THE OCEAN

The side door to the house closes, and I wait as the car backs out of the driveway, I listen for the engine's mechanical murmur easing into silence down the street. Then I double lock the door.

I have a couple of hours alone, so I crouch before the CD cabinet in the living room and try to decide what will it be today: the symphonic jazz of Carlos Martins, the trippy cabaret songs of Rodrigo Leão, the folk buzz of Dazkarieh, or the elegant neoclassical pop music of Madredeus.

These days, I don't listen to Portuguese music unless I'm alone.

I pick a CD of Mário Laginha's piano improvisations, and immediately, on the first cut, "Do Lado de Cá do Mar"—On This Side of the Ocean—a restless baseline of the left hand pushes and pulls at haunting high notes of melody on the right, shifting somewhere between the modal jazz of Miles Davis and an ancestral memory of a Portuguese guitar's ringing tones. As I've learned from my year in Lisbon, Portuguese music doesn't have to be fado to be drenched in *saudade*.

Those odd intervals, shifting from restless to reflective, pluck at something raw inside me, and when the last notes fade to a whisper I jump up and press replay, as I almost always do. Repeating this ritual at five-minute intervals, I sit here on the couch, listening, trying to think it all through. It's my guilty pleasure, my punishment, and I'm not done wallowing yet.

Why Portugal? Maybe the music guided me there. In the wake of my parents' back-to-back deaths in the early 1990s I was ripe for the depths of a fado song's sadness, enough to imagine a connection with that music's country of origin, enough to entertain the silly thought that some distant bloodline reached through the centuries. During a trip to Porto last spring, we visited the port wine lodge founded by Grahams from Glasgow in the nineteenth century. We took the tour and wandered among the stacks of enormous casks, where grapes from the company's vineyard on the upper banks of the Douro River are blended and aged. Though at one point I briefly, stupidly wandered away from the tour group, I felt no hint of ghosts skulking about or any presence that I might recognize and remember from another life. Later we sipped through a wine tasting and visited the gift shop. "Dad, *look*," Hannah called out, pointing in every direction, "everything's Graham!" We bought a couple bottles of the luscious stuff, as well as a Graham's T-shirt, a Graham's cup, a Graham's scarf, a Graham's key chain, and who knows what Graham's else, yet still no lightning bolt of recovered identity struck. Instead, I signed the credit card slip and we returned to our hotel with a slew of Graham's tchotchkes stuffed in our new Graham's tote bag.

Again the notes fade, again I hurry to the CD player, and again I press replay for a song that reminds me of a city where some part of our daughter's childhood was lost and left behind, a song that could be a soundtrack to a ten-word short story written by my friend Gonçalo Tavares: "Um poeta cego pediu mais janelas para a sua casa"—A blind poet ordered more windows for his home. Those few words explain too much of my past year, indulging every view of Portugal I could take in while remaining blind to my child's exhausting struggles to fit in with classmates she at first couldn't speak to, whom she needed to befriend.

There's Alma's key rattling at the two locks on the door, and I hustle to the stereo and turn off Laginha's song in midphrase—I don't want any musical cues reminding Hannah of her difficult year. We're all still raw after these five months since returning from Portugal, and the very air in our home seems bruised, delicate. The side door opens and Hannah strides in from the winter cold, back from volleyball practice, dropping her coat to the floor with typical rough adolescent grace while the melody continues to play inside me.

She scrounges in the pantry for a granola bar, announcing, "I'm so *hungry*," and a more beautiful sentence I have never heard. I still don't understand everything that my daughter has gone through, but I have to shake my head in awe at the strength she used to return to herself and to us. The recovery method Alma and I settled on had its own secret weapon besides soups and smoothies and ever-increasing portions of solid food. The doctors advised us never to argue with our daughter over food but instead to argue with the voice of refusal inside her. So we challenged the unwelcome guiding presence of that voice, allowing Hannah to eventually separate from it, to fight against it with us. And this must have made unconscious sense to her, well aware as she was of Fernando Pessoa and the competing poetic voices of his multiple identities. Some part of Portugal may have undone her, but like a homeopathic cure another part may have helped her rebuild.

Hannah chomps away at her snack and adds, "Milk, I need *milk.*" I try not to stare at her return to athletic energy, and Alma gives me a warning glance to hold in my sloppy emotions—she has her own eye-brimming moments too, of course, but more discipline than I'll ever command. "Let's check the mail," she says. "Wasn't that a package in the mail chute when we drove up?"

Then Alma and Hannah are exclaiming over a well-stamped package from Portugal, a collection of holiday gifts from her friend Sara: photos, earrings, bookmarks, a blouse, and a copy of the CD that Hannah and Sara's chorus recorded with the opera star Teresa Cardoso de Menezes. In short order the CD is out of its case and in the stereo tray, and when Alma and Hannah settle on the couch at first I hesitate. Yet when I sneak a glance at Hannah her eagerness decides me, and I scroll to the first song where the chorus appears, "Se Esse Rua Fosse Minha"—If This Street Were Mine—a popular Brazilian folksong. When we lived in Lisbon I fell hard for a wild, Django Reinhart–inspired rave-up of a version by a local band, O' Que Strada, but here all is slowed and hushed, beginning with the measured plinks of a single harp gently anticipating the singer's crystalline voice, and when the children's chorus finally enters, their voices sound like the hovering spirit of any traveling soul.

I flip through the CD booklet to Hannah's name in the credits, to her face in the chorus photo, a small black-and-white dot of her younger self. I look from this photo to my daughter on the couch, back and forth at this Before and After, until Alma, ever alert, empathetic, and practical, suggests to Hannah, "Why don't you try calling Sara to thank her? It's not too late there."

Off they go to Hannah's computer, and I stay put, booklet still in hand, and push replay. When the children's voices enter with "Se esse rua, esse rua . . ." I'm sure I can hear, at the first high note of "rua," a hint of my daughter's voice. *There* she is, there she *is*, and then Hannah's speaking above the music, her Portuguese still crisp and assured as she strolls into the living room, holding her laptop before her, with Sara on the screen. Hannah points the computer at the window, so her friend can see the snow outside, and then she points it at me. I wave to Sara's image—her face and frame as healthy as Hannah's—on the other side of the ocean. "Boa tarde, Sara," I say, realizing as I speak that it must be evening in Portugal, not afternoon. Before I can correct myself Hannah's rushing up the stairs to show Sara her bedroom, and I push replay again—this is my new favorite song.

When Hannah returns downstairs, her conversation with Sara winds down to back-and-forth exchanges of "adeus" and "beijinhos" before the girls sign off. Then, Hannah's back in the kitchen, asking Alma, "Can we go back to Lisbon this summer? I want to visit Sara, can I?" In the yearning enthusiasm of her voice and Alma's tentative yet willing reply, my own affection for a city I'll never again think of without a pang of sadness begins a wary return, slowly, softly. I can't help shaking my head at these feelings that echo the warmth in the voices of my wife and daughter: even after our recent troubles, Lisbon, the country, the culture still speak to us, and still we listen. So this is *saudade*. Such a complex, contradictory emotion, marked with love and pain, tenderness and longing, just for starters, and mingled in depths I've never understood before and maybe never will.

Again the music fades, and again I press replay.

epilogue

Each morning, we all wake filled with plans that we hope will take us to evening. But our unfolding day rarely fits the neat package we've imagined. How much more do the expectations for a year alter? Life exerts a narrative upon us as we make our way through it.

When *McSweeney's* agreed to give me a go at writing about the year I'd be living abroad with my family in Lisbon, I made the decision to write my periodic dispatches in the present tense, though the ticking clock would be an enemy of this strategy. My choice held a hint of fiction (since I wrote each dispatch days or weeks, and eventually months after the events described), yet was mainly a method of truth, an attempt to evoke the intensity of each moment that is so typical of encountering another culture, the internal shaping that travel applies to us.

The dispatches soon became their own developing narrative, real events creating the plot of a story I wrote down without knowing where it would end. With the uncanny feeling that my family and I were unfinished characters in an as yet unwritten tale, I balanced the stories of exploring the city of Lisbon with our past travels to Africa, my wife's new research among Cape Verdeans, my daughter's year of Portuguese schooling, and the bumpy road of parenthood.

Yet what I wrote, the choices I made of what might capture my attention, influenced not only what I was able to see but also what I was unable to see of those continuing, unfolding tales. The writer Grace Paley has often said that there's always a story behind the story, and that hidden story turned out to be the drama of my daughter's immersion in another culture, complicating her first steps from childhood to adolescence. How imperfectly I understood the epic battle within her. When my family's troubles erupted, I abandoned these dispatches, abandoned the idea of ever writing another, much less collect them in book form. But as Hannah healed, everyone— Alma, Nathaniel, Hannah—urged me to continue writing, to finish the story, to add to its joy its secret sorrow.

I hope the honesty of this telling will alert others to the difficulties of taking a child along to another country. Most children are primed for brief vacations—two weeks' rush through a foreign country can easily be enjoyed, or at least endured. But in the words of my son Nathaniel, living a year abroad with children is "academia's great fantasy," an assumption that the richness of the experience itself will be a gift to one's child. It's an assumption that is rarely questioned. Yet weeks turning into months or more away from home pose exponential challenges that must be faced beforehand and throughout the extended stay, to ensure that the gift is worth giving.

So, does sorrow erase the joy of travel, or does the story of this epilogue have its own epilogue? Hannah still longs for Lisbon, as if the fire inside her has glazed and burnished her love of the city. At her insistence, she returned in the summer of 2008 to visit her friend Sara for ten days, and we hope to make this a yearly ritual. Hannah speaks constantly of living in Portugal again, perhaps as an exchange student in either high school or college. "I think about Lisbon every day," she tells us. "I can't wait to go back."

εnd noτεs/mini-dispaτcHεs

I DON'T KNOW WHY I LOVE LISBON

Page 4: The wait staff in any Portuguese eating establishment are a fairly no-nonsense bunch. Order your meal and they will get it to you efficiently but rarely with a smile. There's little or no attempt to be the customer's buddy, no false friendliness. This professional ethos of invisibility goes both ways: you can linger over your meal as long as you like, no matter how busy the restaurant may be, and even if you're covered in cobwebs the staff will still leave you alone, unless you order another jar of wine or a cup of espresso. There's no postprandial hurry to pry you from the table. You could sit there forever, contemplating the end of the universe, until you say the magic words "A conta, faz favor"—The check, please.

365 DAYS OF PORK SURPRISE

Page 16: Pork continues to stalk my wife. When she trolls through a Lisbon department store's online catalog and finds an office chair she likes, the sleek beige seat and backing of the chair turns out to be made of *pele de porco*—pigskin. In a café's menu she sees a ham and cheese sandwich listed as "pão Deus mista"—God's sandwich. Our cookbook includes a recipe for Toucinho do Abade de Priscos—the Abbott of Prisco's Pudding—which sports as ingredients egg yolks and sugar, lemon, sweet wine, and a hefty chunk of fatty ham. Alma can't bring herself to say it, but I can: "ham pudding." There's even a children's TV show called *A Cidade dos Porcos*—The City of Pigs ("Numa cidade, três porquinhos viven divertidas situações"—In a city, three little piggies encounter amusing adventures—the program guide confides). It's the half hour just before *Os Simpsons*.

Every day requires vigilance. In one of the larger local groceries, when a succulent roll of meat laced with tasty bits of vegetables is featured, tantalizingly, in the beef section, Alma—sensitized to the lurking possibilities of pork—asks the butcher if this really is beef.

"All beef," he replies, slightly taken aback by her question. This may be a promising response, but Alma has learned to be specific, very specific.

"There's no pork inside?"

"Pork? Only the layer of fat and some bits of *chorizo*; otherwise, it's all beef."

ALCHEMY: FROM A RUBE TO A LOCAL

Page 21: "Inch by inch I conquered the inner terrain I was born with," Pessoa once wrote, adding, "I gave birth to my infinite being, but I had to wrench myself out of me with forceps." His multifaceted "myself" included Alberto Caeiro, Ricardo Reis, and Álvaro de Campos (he wrote scores of less developed alter egos), and not only did each heteronym create a distinctive poetry, but Reis and de Campos even wrote critical essays commenting on Caiero's poetry (Bernardo Soares, the prose poet nominally responsible for *The Book of Disquiet*, was considered by Pessoa to be a semi-heteronym, because their personalities were too similar). Only once was Pessoa tempted to add a real person to the extended family of himself—Orphélia Queiroz. He eventually ended their relationship by using one of his heteronyms, Álvaro de Campos, to write her a breakup letter.

Pessoa always believed he would be famous, and after his death a trunk in his apartment was found containing thousands of unpublished pages deserving of his self-confidence. I think he would have enjoyed the knick-knackified proliferation of his image (or images, if you count his heteronyms: a popular rendering is of Pessoa in profile, with four identical profiles dogging behind). Besides coffee and espresso cups, key chains and T-shirts, you can find his face on notebooks, bookmarks, *azulejos*, even Do Not Disturb door signs. Child-friendly biographies of Pessoa's life and editions of his work appear regularly, and rarely a day passes without a mention, in Portugal's newspapers or magazines, of Pessoa's work and literary legacy. His tomb now rests in the Mosteiro dos Jerónimos in Belém (Portugal's equivalent of Great Britain's Westminster Abbey). In one of the cloister's alcoves stands a rectangular obelisk, and on one marble side is carved a poem written by Pessoa while the other three sides feature poems by his heteronyms.

The Portuguese deeply get this guy. The beginning of our first family trip to Lisbon, back in June 1999, coincided with the 111th anniversary of Pessoa's birth, celebrated by a big bash open to the public. What luck! Newbies, we wandered up and down the Bairro Alto; Hannah, just turned four, tired quickly, so I carried her on my shoulders. Finally we found the party crowded in a smallish space, everyone gawking at one long wall covered with identically sized squares of paintings, organized in a grid. Four hundred Portuguese artists had been asked to contribute a work of art about Pessoa, all of them meant to add up as a single portrait of the poet. We made our way through the happy gathering, and with Hannah still perched on my shoulders (enjoying the novel views) I managed to accept hors d'oeuvres and then a glass of wine as I examined the marvelous wall. The artwork illustrated scenes or images from Pessoa's writing, repeated favorite lines from his poems, made playful variations on the iconic details of his hat, glasses, and mustache: the poet sitting at his desk with multiple echoing shadows behind him; Pessoa in a toga—his hat and glasses still on—dancing in a forest with Botticelli's Three Graces; an actual Ken doll, his face appropriately Pessoa'd up, and on his plastic chest an arrow-through-the-heart tattoo with Orphélia's name printed just beneath; an empty pair of glasses floating above Pessoa's last recorded words: "I don't know what tomorrow will bring." We would have lingered for a while, but when someone broke out an accordion and the crowd sang along to his playing—the lyrics probably from one of Pessoa's poems—suddenly the party felt more private, something particularly Portuguese that we couldn't quite enter, so we quietly slipped away.

ISN'T THERE A LAW AGAINST FILCHING A *CALÇADA*?

Page 37: Why this sudden expansion of the tiny breadbox of officially sanctioned names? In the past decade or so, Portugal has experienced for the first time in centuries an increase in immigration. Drawn by the country's relative uptick in European Union wealth, immigrants from Brazil, Cape Verde, Angola, and the other former colonies of the former empire have settled in Portugal, which has also become a favored destination of immigrants from Romania and Ukraine. As new Portuguese citizens are born of these parents, suddenly the standard monikers José and Maria don't quite cut it, and now they have to rub elbows with the likes of Adiel, Herédia, Evangelino, and Lira. The Direcçao-Geral dos Registos e Notariado has been a bit stingy, though: only eighteen new names have been approved. Count on more names to follow in future years.

THOSE TRICKY SUBGESTURES

Page 48: A few months after my encounter with Saramago, I'm renting a car for a trip into the country, and of course the clerk's English is better than my Portuguese, so we quickly revert to the world's current lingua franca. One topic of conversation leads to another, and as I'm expressing my enthusiasm for the culture and literature of Portugal I can't help mentioning Saramago's less than pleased appraisal when we met.

Chagrined, the clerk says, "That's just Saramago, a difficult man sometimes. We're not like that; the Portuguese welcome everyone. We don't care if you're white or black, where you come from or what your religion is, we welcome everyone." He pauses, as if taking a breath, and then adds, "Except the Gypsies. Watch out for them—you can't trust the Gypsies." On he goes about their skills at deception while I force a stiff smile, wishing I could put the brakes on this disappointing rant.

Later I discover that Quaresma, one of the best soccer players on the first place Porto team, is a Gypsy. I've admired his elegant risks on the pitch as much as I've been annoyed by his haircut: a strange little ridge of hair that runs from crown to nape like a tiny Stegosaurus back plate, shaped by a finger or two of grease. It's a popular cut, with adolescent boys everywhere sporting it, a silly look just waiting to be out of date. But now that I know he's the Gypsy Jackie Robinson of Portuguese soccer, I forgive him his weird do.

NEARLY THE SAME SUBSTANCE

Page 55: Besides the many thousands of families who lost a son, brother, father, or husband in Salazar's long and unpopular colonial wars, there's another group of Portuguese with complicated African connections: the *retornados*—those half million Portuguese who, after living on that continent for generations, left when the colonies gained independence in the mid-1970s. They're a significant portion of the country's population, and rarely a week goes by when we don't meet a Portuguese man or woman who was born in Africa or whose parents, uncle, aunt, or grandparents lived there, and they're always willing to wax nostalgic for a long minute or two—another version of *saudade*.

GO, WATCHAMACALITS!

Page 57: *Os Três* is short for *Os Três Grandes*—The Big Three. For some cynical local souls, they're really *Os Chamados Três Grandes*—The So-Called Big Three—because the Portuguese aren't easily impressed with themselves. No longer major players in world politics and off the beaten track in a corner of Europe, the Portuguese somehow balance an uneasy mix of pride in their culture with an inferiority complex. Often I meet Portuguese who are shocked that I'm even aware of their literature, music, food, let alone love it all. There must be something wrong with me, they seem to think but don't say. "So why did you choose to live in Lisbon?" I'm often asked in a barely muted incredulous tone that contains the pointed subtext "What *is* the matter with you?"

Once, at a party in a Lisbon restaurant, I remarked offhandedly that Spanish culture doesn't interest me, and I felt a little charge ripple through the people nearby, as if they were about to heave me in the air, as if I were the fellow who'd scored a winning goal, but of course, being polite and deceptively restrained Portuguese, they did no such thing.

CHAMA-ME ISHMAIL

Page 66: The wide range of Portuguese history and empire is available at almost every street corner, if you only know how to look. One spring day as Alma and I sit at a café's sidewalk table, I notice that the facades of the lower floors of the buildings on either side of the street are decorated with *azulejos*—those tiles painted with geometric patterns that are a legacy of the country's Moorish past—while the upper floors embody the blocky architectural style of Salazar's Estado Novo. At our feet, of course, stretch thousands, millions, of *calçadas*, the cobblestone reminders of when Portugal served as the eastern edge of the Roman world. Three young men at the table beside us speak Portuguese with what must be an Angolan or Mozambican accent, and then I notice, as our pot of tea arrives, our waiter's Brazilian accent. Across the street a South Asian couple walks by, trying to manage a muted public argument, and though I'm too far away to hear, I imagine that they're trading disappointments in Portuguese, their ancestors hailing from the former colony of Goa. A little later a middle-aged Chinese woman strides by with unusual stilettoed confidence (why, I wonder, does no one wearing high heels ever twist an ankle on these cobblestone sidewalks?), carrying on in Portuguese into her cell phone, and I think: Macau. By now Alma and I search for competing new examples, and she points out a sign beside the door of a professional building, where the lawyers and doctors listed have names like Cardoso, Cabral, Oliveira, all names that were adopted by Jews who were forcibly converted to Christianity in the fifteenth century. Then I call attention to the Campo Pequeno bullfighting ring, visible at one end of the street, its impressive blue domes influenced by Muslim architecture. Not to be outdone, Alma reminds me of the glossy shopping mall and food court that recently opened below the ring, a sign of Portugal's European Union–inspired consumer culture. At this point I feel a little dizzy in this jumbled-up history text of a street, but I think I understand better now why Fernando Pessoa was able to nurture his many selves, as he walked to work each day through Lisbon's palimpsest of realities.

ANOTHER HISTORY LESSON

Page 75: On April 25 we take the subway to the Marquis de Pombal station and meet with our friends Fernanda and Luís for the independence day celebration. Together we stroll down the Avenida da Liberdade—a lovely thoroughfare bordered by tall, thin plane trees that create a canopy a hundred feet above us—and wait for the parade to begin on this crisp, clear day. But first we all have to buy long-stemmed carnations in remembrance of the flowers young *lisboetas* gratefully placed in the guns of soldiers during the bloodless revolution of 1974.

Soon the parade is in full swing, with the drumming and singing of costumed regional folklore ensembles alternating with slogan chanting by political groups. This parade seems as much protest as celebration, and what could be a healthier sign of democracy? Fernanda and Luís are great hosts. An anthropologist who works with Cape Verdeans in Lisbon and the United Kingdom, Luís offers sardonic cultural commentary while Fernanda, a linguist and journalist, offers backstage gossip on the political personalities and helps us translate some of the banners. O GOVERNO ENCERRA SERVIÇOS E ENGORDA OS PRIVADOS—The government closes services and fattens the private sector—declares a huge screen depicting Prime Minister José Sócrates as a groveling corporate lackey. A gay and lesbian rights group carries the banner SE O 25 DE ABRIL TROUXE A LIBERDADE, ONDE ESTA A NOSSA IGUALADADE?—If April 25th brought liberty, where is our equality? A student organization waves the warning A LUTA NÃO ACABOU. FASCISMO NUNCA MAIS—The fight isn't over; never again fascism.

Despite the feisty nature of some of the banners, everyone's having a good time, and the drum brigades' rhythms echo nicely off the avenue's buildings. The Movimento Democrático de Mulheres marches by, sporting a banner for peace and equality, then an immigrants' organization follows, asking for the same. Just as the parade begins winding down, a strong wind ripples through the plane trees, which, ripe for spring renewal, let loose above us clouds of pollen, nasty stuff that sticks to hair and clothes and soon has nearly everyone coughing. It's as if the spirit of Salazar has returned to unleash tormenting demons in the air, and the crowds start a swift trek into cafés or down subway entrances. Because Hannah has a lot of homework, she and Alma head for the subway too, but I decide to continue with Fernanda and Luís to a restaurant that displays in the window a handwritten sign, "Há Caracóis," which, roughly translated, means "We Have Snails."

They're the season's specialty. Steamed in garlicky butter, they come out from the kitchen piled in a mound on a large plate, and all that's needed is a toothpick or minifork to nab a tender body from a tiny shell. We order beer, joke and laugh in a mixture of English and Portuguese (mostly English, for my sake), and watch through the wide window as people still hustle down the street fleeing gusts of pollen. But we have time to wait out any evil spirits, so we order a bottle of *vinho verde* and one more plate of snails.

LIGHT FOR LIGHT

Page 92: I first met Rui at an international short story conference held in Lisbon, where he read his story "The Writing Bug," a dystopian lament about a world gone wild with writing mania: "All my friends write. Great. All my friends love to write. Fantastic. Even I don't dislike writing, though I no longer do it. Ah, to write! To write words. To write things. To write the world. The world inside us. And the world outside us. All my friends write. All my friends are writers. All my friends produce books. And it's not just my friends, it's everyone else as well. My neighbors write poems, the waitress at the café writes detective novels, the bank employee writes love stories and the grocer writes historical romances . . ."

The editor of the literary magazine *Hunger Mountain* had asked me to pull together a section on contemporary Portuguese fiction if I found enough worthy examples while at the conference, and I knew at once that this story would make the cut. After Rui's reading I cornered him with praise and asked if I could publish his story, and after the briefest squint of hesitation, before I could further explain myself, he said to this absolute stranger, "Sure," and so began our friendship.

Page 98: Ninety-eight percent of the movies in the video store that serves our apartment complex come from the United States, though here they're all subtitled. The shop is pretty much up to date on the latest releases, with the same stinkers that are available at any Blockbuster back home—sad, nearly straight-to-video Hillary Duff castoffs; horror-torture fests that give off their own distinctive pall in a back corner of the store; sentimental date flicks that should come with a diabetes warning; and manic animated films filled with trash-talking animals. One of the reasons we moved abroad was the hope of getting away from this sort of stuff, but it seems there's no escape. Still, a decent video is a good way to kill an evening or reward Hannah for her usual excellent grades, but whenever we roam the store's aisles I feel like a foreign undercover agent, come to check that the latest cultural poison is available for the unsuspecting local populace.

THREE CHURCHES

Page 112: After a good bit of back-and-forth, a memorial to the victims of the São Domingos massacre was unanimously approved by the Lisbon city council in early 2008 (probably during a pause in that august body's usual internecine political warfare). Months later, a modest commemorative sculpture was placed before the church—502 years to the day after the tragedy, but better late than never.

PARTICLE AND WAVE

Page 118: Because *atropedalo*—run over—is a word that comes up a lot in the local newspapers, the Associaçao dos Cidadaos Auto-mobilizados works mightily to educate the public about driving safety. Rui Zink, a member of ACAM, has written, in a blog posting titled "We Are the Champions, My Friends," about a recent twenty-four-hour period when Hamas and Fatah rivalries caused only four deaths while at the same time eight people died on Portuguese roads.

Page 118: The best present I receive on Dia do Pai (the early spring Portuguese version of Father's Day) is a gift I'd been pining for: the *Atlas Arquitectura de Lisboa*, a coffee table–friendly volume filled with aerial photos and elegant, crisply rendered maps of fifty-six selected areas of the city. It's a book that outmaps Google Maps. Each section provides a brief history of the neighborhood, even the names of the responsible urban planners; the number of floors every building has and how high each block is above sea level; which surfaces are paved and which are grassy, which spaces are public, which private. And the detail!—even individual trees in small parks and *praças* are noted. It's hard to explain the thrill of discovering in a map of our neighborhood the exact replicated pattern of the cobbled walkway in our apartment complex's garden. After hours of careful (Alma would say obsessive) study, when I lift my eyes from the large pages

I've found a new neighborhood worth exploring during our next long day of writing.

Page 124: The prestige of writers in Portugal can exhibit itself in the most unexpected places, even at the last home game of Os Belenenses (nicknamed Os Azuis—The Blues), the soccer team whose stadium lies three blocks down from our apartment. Os Azuis are playing Marítimo, a team from the island of Madeira. While Marítimo is stuck in the league's lower rankings, Os Azuis are having a stellar year: starting nearly in the basement, they're now tied for fourth place. Alma, Hannah, and I arrive at the ticket stand fully loaded with euros, but we're told the entrance fee has been waived. A free game! This probably explains the unusually large crowd lining up to enter the stadium, and I'm guessing half of them are here for the first time. I've attended a few games since early August's pre-season, so I can't help feeling a little smug, and I savor the memory of one late fall fiasco of a match during a hard dreary rain, when Os Azuis and the visiting team spent the last half sliding over the slick wet grass of the pitch.

Back then, almost nobody came to cheer, but now that Dady—the pride of the Cape Verdean community in Lisbon—is one goal shy of the league's leader, and Nivaldo—who brings in the Brazilian fans—is one of the best defensive players of the year, you can't keep people away. Because of the size of this eager crowd, there's a larger than usual police presence frisking the incoming for any sharp or possibly trigger-ready means of expressing team support. As I'm patted down, the guard feels something suspicious in my coat pocket. It's just a pen, but he looks it over carefully—after all, I might use this to poke some hapless Marítimo fan's eye out. "Sou escritor"—I'm a writer—I explain. When the guard replies silently with a skeptical "I dunno" stare, I do a little Rolodex whirl of the pages of my notebook, clearly rife with my left-handed scrawl, and he switches his face from dubious to respectful and waves me through.

FAIRLY MEDIEVAL

Page 128: Though Portuguese is the sixth most common language in the world and the official language of eight countries, the originating European brand serves only ten million speakers, so in order to get on in the world the Portuguese feel compelled to learn, besides English, more than a little French, German, and Spanish. The Portuguese give themselves a head start by adding subtitles to every TV show and movie that comes from another country: no dubbed voices for them. Even from a young age Portuguese are used to hearing foreign languages spoken regularly, and instantly translated at the bottom of the screen, which gives them one step up in any linguistic showdown.

ON THIS SIDE OF THE OCEAN

Page 143: The Maudsley Method, developed in England, has accomplished a 90 percent recovery rate for eating disorders among adolescent girls and boys, an astounding improvement over other therapies. Relatively new to the United States, this family-based method has rapidly grown in popularity among doctors and is now offered through medical centers at the University of Chicago, Stanford University, and Columbia University, among many others. The best book to consult for this method is *Help Your Teenager Beat an Eating Disorder*, by James Lock and Daniel Le Grange.

Page 144: *Saudade*'s complexities sometimes remind me of José Saramago's concept of the fine-print emotional nuances of subgestures. Yet the more I think on it, *saudade* seems like the act of creation itself. Once the original moment of inspiration is over, an artist can't keep him- or herself from returning to that still unfinished story, poem, essay, novel, canvas, or musical theme. The task of revising—rethinking, returning again and again to worry and shape what was begun in the past—is an experience of *saudade*. Whatever form it eventually takes, a work of art is *saudade* with results.

SOURCES OF
LITERATURE QUOTED

Fernando Pessoa quotes are from *The Book of Disquiet*, translated by Richard Zenith (Penguin Classics, 2003).

Mia Couto quotes are from *Sleepwalking Land*, translated by David Brookshaw (Serpent's Tail, 2006).

Ana Hatherly quote is from the poem "Um golem alugado," from the collection *O pavão negro* (Assírio & Alvim, 2003); unauthorized attempt at translation by Philip Graham.

José Saramago quote is from *The Double*, translated by Margaret Jull Costa (Harcourt, 2004).

Excerpt from the poem "Canto da chávena de chá," by Fiama Hasse Pais Brandão, is from *Cantos do canto* (Relógio D'Agua Editores, 1995); awkward English translation committed by Philip Graham.

Excerpt from the poem "Drift," by Sophia de Mello Breyner, is from *Log Book: Selected Poems*, translated by Richard Zenith (Carcanet, 1997).

Textbook quotations are from *Á descoberta da história e geografia de Portugal*, vol. 2, *6 ano*, by Maria Luísa Santos, Claudia Amaral, and Lídia Maia (Porto Editora, 2006).

Leo Tolstoy quote is from *Anna Karenina*, translated by Constance Garnett (Modern Library, [1934]).

Quotations from the work of Miguel Torga are from *Tales and More Tales from the Mountains*, translated by Ivana Rangel-Carlsen (Carcanet, 1995).

Quotations from the work of Gil Vicente are from *The Boat Plays*, translated by David Johnston (Oberon Books, 1997).

Excerpt from the work of Pedro Tamen is from *Honey and Poison: Selected Poems*, translated by Richard Zimler (Carcanet, 2001).

Grace Paley quote is from the short story "A Conversation with My Father," from *Enormous Changes at the Last Minute* (Farrar, Straus and Giroux, 1974).

Gonçalo Tavares's short story "Exigência" was first published in *Diário de Notícias*, April 23, 2007; translation offered with humility by Philip Graham.

Excerpt from the story "The Writing Bug," by Rui Zink, translated by Richard Zenith, was published in *Hunger Mountain*, no. 9, Fall 2006, in the section "'A Book, Open Wide, in Our Hands': Contemporary Portuguese Writing," edited by Philip Graham.